Editor: Barbara Taylor
Designer: Ben White
Consultant: Terry Cash
Illustrators: Kuo Kang Chen, Peter Bull

Kingfisher Books, Grisewood & Dempsey Ltd,
Elsley House, 24–30 Great Titchfield Street, London W1P 7AD

First published in 1987 by Kingfisher Books.
The material in this book has previously been published
in paperback by Kingfisher Books (1987) in four
separate volumes – Fun With Science:
Water, Air, Moving, Light

Reprinted 1988 (twice), 1989

BRITISH LIBRARY CATALOGUING IN PUBLICATION DATA
Walpole, Brenda
Fun with science.
1. Science —— Experiments —— Juvenile
literature
I. Title
507'.24 Q163

ISBN 0-86272-241-1

Phototypeset by Tradespools Ltd, Frome, Somerset
Colour separations by Scantrans pte Ltd, Singapore
Printed by South China Printing Company, Hong Kong

KINGFISHER

FUN WITH SCIENCE

EXPERIMENTS • TRICKS • THINGS TO MAKE

BRENDA WALPOLE

KINGFISHER BOOKS

Contents

Moving

Light

Before you start

This book is full of simple science experiments that will help you to discover more about how things work and why things happen in the world around you. The four sections – Water, Air, Moving and Light – are each divided into a number of topics. Where a new topic begins, there is a blue line around the edge of the page.

You will be able to find most of the equipment you need for your experiments around your home. You do not need expensive equipment to be a good scientist.

A word of warning

Some science experiments can be dangerous. Ask an adult to help you with difficult hammering or cutting and any experiments that involve flames, hot liquids or chemicals. Don't forget to put out any flames and turn off the heat when you have finished. Good scientists avoid accidents.

How to be a good scientist

- Collect all the equipment you need before you start.
- Keep a notebook. Write down what you do in your experiments and what happens.
- Watch your experiments carefully. Sometimes things happen very quickly and you may have to try a test more than once.

- If your experiment does not work properly the first time, try again or try doing it in a different way until you succeed.
- If your answers are not exactly the same as those in the book, do not worry. It does not mean that you are wrong. See if you can work out what has happened and why.

Finding out more

- Make small changes in the design of your equipment to see if the results are still the same.
- Make up your own experiments to test your ideas about how things work.
- Look out for examples of the scientific ideas described in this book around your home and out of doors.
- Do not worry if you do not understand all the things you see – there are always new things to discover. Remember that many of the most famous scientific discoveries were made by accident (see pages 92 and 116).

WATER

This section of the book will help you to investigate water. Think about water when you drink or wash or when it rains.

There are six main topics in this section:

- Water as a liquid, a solid and a gas
- Water levels and flowing water
- Surface tension
- Density and displacement
- Dissolving substances in water
- Water for life and power

Use the symbols below to help you identify the three kinds of practical activities in this book.

EXPERIMENTS

TRICKS

THINGS TO MAKE

Introduction

Water is a remarkable substance. It covers more than two-thirds of the Earth's surface and no life on Earth could survive without it. Most of the experiments in this book will help you to investigate the amazing characteristics of liquid water. You can take a close look at water's stretchy 'skin', discover why heavy ships float in water and find out how some substances disappear when they are mixed with water. You can also find out how liquid water is used to turn the machinery that produces the electricity in hydro-electric power stations.

But liquid water is only one of the three forms in which water can exist. If water is cooled to 0°C, it freezes to become a solid called ice. If it is heated to 100°C, it boils and disappears into the air as a gas called water vapour.

As you come to understand the different characteristics of water you will be able to answer the questions on these two pages and explain how water influences the way in which things happen in the world around you.

◀Why do some substances disappear when you mix them with water? (p. 40—41)

▲Why does an ice cube float in water and an iceberg float in the sea? (pages 16—17)

▼ Why do some objects float and others sink? (pages 32—33)

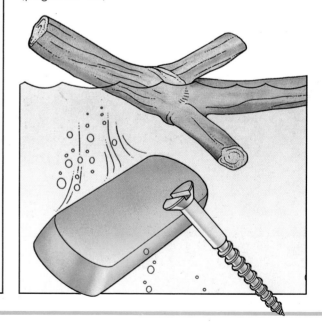

▲ What makes clouds form in the sky?
Why are clouds different shapes? (pages 14–15)

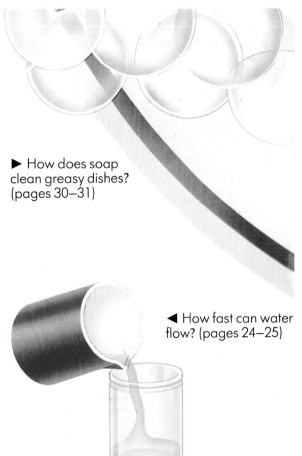

► How does soap clean greasy dishes? (pages 30–31)

▼ Why does water always settle on a horizontal level? (pages 20–21)

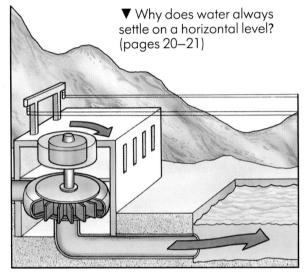

◄ How fast can water flow? (pages 24–25)

▲ How is water used to produce electricity? (pages 46–47)

► Where do snow and ice come from? (pages 16–17)

▼ Why do ships float in water?
How much cargo can they hold? (pages 34–35)

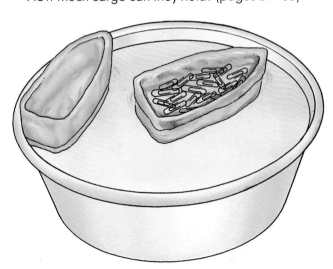

Disappearing Water

When it rains, water falls from the sky and collects in puddles on the ground. But after the rain has stopped and the Sun begins to shine, the puddles dry up and the water disappears. Where does all the water go? The heat of the Sun makes the water turn into tiny droplets, which rise up into the air. This process is called **evaporation** and the droplets are called **water vapour**.

▶In hot countries, fruit is left out in the Sun to dry. The water in the fruit slowly turns into water vapour and evaporates into the air. This helps to preserve the fruit so it can be stored and used later.

Investigate Evaporation

Equipment: Two jars (the same shape and size), tin foil, a marker pen.

1. Fill the two jars about half full of water. Check the water level is the same in both jars and mark the level on the outside.
2. Make a foil cover for one of the jars.
3. Leave both jars in a warm place for a few days. Then check the water levels again. Which jar has less water in it?

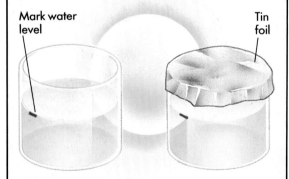

Mark water level

Tin foil

How it works
The heat makes the water evaporate in both jars. But the foil cover stops the water vapour escaping into the air so the level of water remains higher in this jar.

Drying the Washing

How quickly does water evaporate from objects and make them dry out? Try these investigations to find the best drying conditions.

Cut a piece of cloth into six pieces — make them all about the same size. Wet all the cloths.
- Put one in the sun and one in the shade.
- Hang one in a breeze and one in still air.
- Leave one folded or squashed into a ball and spread one out flat.

Which piece of cloth dries first?

Make Your Own Refrigerator

One way to keep things cool is to cover them with a clay pot (such as a tall flower pot), which you have soaked in water. As water evaporates from the clay pot it takes heat away so the object underneath will remain cool. If you stand the pot in a bowl of water, it will soak up more water as it dries out and your 'fridge' will last longer.

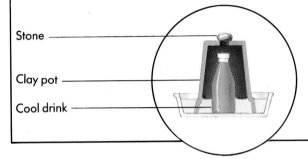

Stone ——————

Clay pot ——————

Cool drink ——————

Water evaporates most rapidly in a warm, sunny place. A breeze carries away the water vapour that evaporates from the surface of the cloth and this helps the cloth to dry. Spreading out the cloth also makes it dry faster as water can evaporate from the whole surface. So the best time to dry the washing is in warm, windy weather and the clothes will dry faster if they are spread out.

More things to try
Compare different materials, such as artificial and natural fabrics. Put them in the same place and see which one of them dries first.

Keeping Cool

Why do you feel cold when you get out of a warm bath? This is because water evaporates from your skin and takes heat away with it. The same process helps you to cool down if you get very hot, for example if you run in a race. Sweat escapes from pores in your skin and evaporates to cool you down.

Water from Air

Water vapour does not always stay in the air. It sometimes turns back into liquid water again. This is called **condensation** and it happens when air cools down. Cold air cannot hold as much water vapour as warm air so some of the water vapour condenses to form tiny drops of liquid water. The white trails made by high-flying aircraft are formed as a result of condensation.

Making Water Appear

Put a glass of water in the refrigerator for an hour or so until it is quite cold. When you take it out, you will see drops of water forming on the sides of the glass.

How it works
The cold glass cools the air around it and some of the water vapour condenses to form drops of water on the sides of the glass. This is why you may see water droplets running down the inside of misty window panes on cold days.

What is Steam?

The steam from a boiling kettle forms as water vapour escapes from the hot water inside and meets the colder air outside. Tiny drops of liquid water condense from the vapour and join together until they are big enough for you to see as clouds of steam.

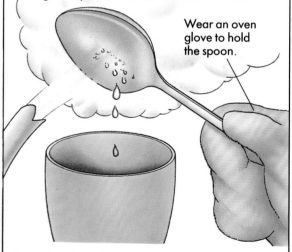

Wear an oven glove to hold the spoon.

If you hold a cold spoon in the steam, the water vapour will condense and drip off.
Warning: Take care; steam is very hot and could burn you.

Why Does it Rain?

Heat from the Sun makes the liquid water in oceans, rivers and lakes evaporate and water vapour rises into the air. At very high levels, the air is too cold to hold all the vapour.

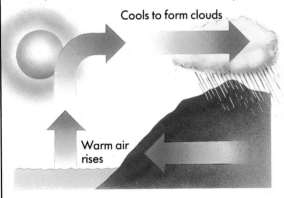

Cools to form clouds

Warm air rises

Clouds begin to form as the water vapour condenses in the cold air to form drops of water. The drops stay in the clouds until they get too heavy to hang in the air. When that happens, they fall as rain.

Heap clouds

Wispy clouds

Layer clouds

Look out for three main cloud shapes. Fluffy, heap clouds (cumulus) mean fine weather but may grow into huge, grey storm clouds later on. Layer clouds (stratus) bring rain or snow. Wispy clouds (cirrus) are so high they are made of ice crystals.

Make a Rain Gauge

All you need to measure the rainfall in your area is a clear plastic bottle and a ruler. Cut the top off the bottle and fit it upside down into the rest of the bottle to form a funnel. Use the ruler to mark a scale on the side of the bottle.

Set up your rain gauge in an open place – not under trees where drops of water from the trees might fall in. Fix it firmly in the ground and keep it out of the wind so that it is not blown over and the wind does not blow the raindrops away from the funnel.

Check the amount of rain that falls each day and make your own rainfall chart. Remember to empty the bottle each day after you have filled in your chart.

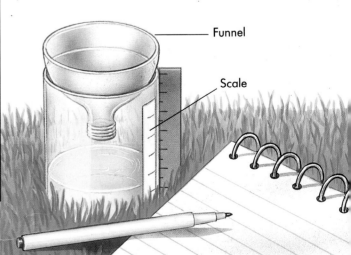

Funnel

Scale

Frozen Solid

Water is a remarkable substance because it can exist in three different forms – as a liquid, as a gas (water vapour) and as a solid (ice). On the next four pages, you can find out more about solid water and how to use its special properties in some simple tricks and experiments. Solid water can form in two ways. The first is when liquid water cools to 0°C (32°F) – its 'freezing point'. This is how ice cubes form. The second is when water vapour freezes – this is how the 'frost' forms in a freezer.

Floating Ice

As water freezes and changes to ice, it expands and takes up more space than it did as liquid water. This makes the ice lighter than the liquid water it was made from and so it floats – but only just. Because ice takes up about one ninth more space than it does as liquid water, about one ninth of an iceberg shows above the water. There is nine times as much below the surface.

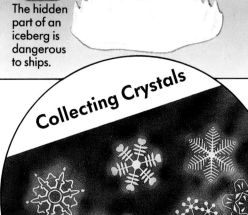

The hidden part of an iceberg is dangerous to ships.

Looking for Ice

During the winter, look for the different shapes and patterns that frozen water can make.
- Snowflakes form when water vapour freezes.
- Icicles form when water drips in very cold air.
- Ice crystals make patterns on cold window panes when water vapour freezes slowly.
- Sheets of ice cover the surfaces of puddles, pails, tubs and ponds.

Collecting Crystals

Catch snowflakes on a piece of black cloth or card that has been kept in a refrigerator – this helps to stop the snowflakes melting. Use a magnifying glass to examine them. Each one is different but they all have six sides!

 ## Ice Needs Space

Float an ice cube in a glass of water. What do you think will happen when the ice cube melts? Will the glass overflow?

When the ice cube melts, the level of water in the glass stays about the same. This is because the water from the ice takes up less space than the ice itself.

Equipment: A small bottle made of glass or thick plastic – about the same size as the bottles used for food colouring.

1. Fill the bottle to the brim with water and make a loose-fitting cap out of tin foil. Put the bottle in the freezer and leave it until the water has frozen hard.

2. When you look at it again, you will see that the ice has pushed up the cap.

How it works

Ice takes up more space than the water that froze to make it. This is why pipes may burst in winter. The water inside them expands as it freezes and forces the joints apart or makes the pipes split.

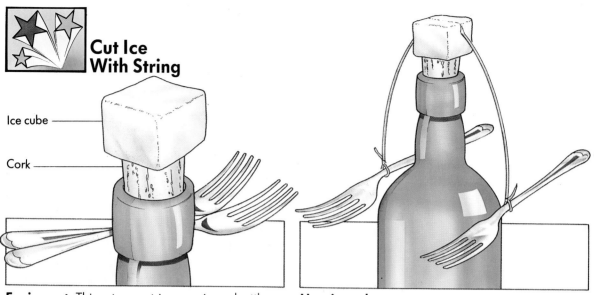

Cut Ice With String

Ice cube —

Cork —

Equipment: Thin, strong string or wire, a bottle with a cork, a cube of ice, two heavy forks.

1. Push the cork into the bottle so that about 2.5 cm (1 inch) sticks out. Balance the ice cube on top of the cork.

2. Cut a piece of string or wire about 40 cm (1 foot 4 inches) long and tie one fork to each end. Hang the string over the ice cube. Put the bottle in the refrigerator. The string will pass through the ice without dividing it into two.

How it works
The pressure of the string or wire makes the ice melt just below it. Water forms under the string or wire and it slides down through the ice. The ice freezes again just above the string or wire.

This is what happens when people skate on ice. Their weight presses on the ice and makes it melt under the blades of the skates. The layer of water helps the skates to glide over the ice. The water freezes again afterwards.

Houses of Ice

The Inuit (Eskimo) people of Canada used to build houses out of ice to live in when they went on hunting trips, These houses (called igloos) were built from blocks of frozen snow, which were placed on top of each other to make a dome-shaped hut. The gaps between the blocks were filled with loose snow and a hole was left in the top for air to get in and out. Heat from a stove inside made the walls begin to melt. Opening the door made this liquid water freeze to form a layer of ice, which stopped heat escaping.

Today, very few Inuit build traditional igloos or make long hunting journeys across the ice.

Lift Ice With a Matchstick

Equipment: A bowl of water, an ice cube, a matchstick, some salt.

Float the ice cube in the bowl of water and lay the matchstick carefully on the top of the cube. Then sprinkle a little salt around the matchstick. Soon it will be frozen into the ice cube and you will be able to use the matchstick to lift the ice.

How it works

When you sprinkle salt onto the ice cube, it makes the ice around the matchstick melt. This is because salt water freezes at a lower temperature than ordinary water. In other words, it has to get colder than 0°C (32°F) before salt water will freeze. But no salt falls under the matchstick and it becomes frozen into the ice. This allows you to lift the ice with the matchstick.

Salt is spread on roads in the winter to melt the ice. The salty water that is left does not freeze until the temperature is well below 0°C. Adding anti-freeze to the water in car radiators is another way to stop water freezing. A mixture of the two liquids will not freeze until minus 30°C (minus 22°F).

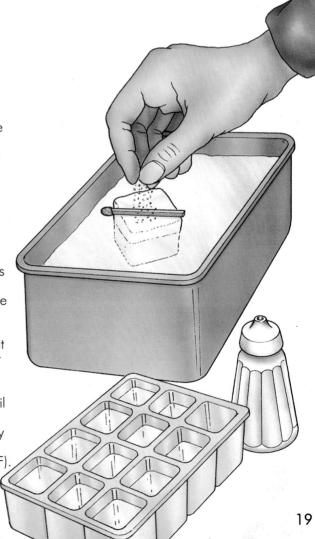

On the Level

Water (and everything else on Earth) is pulled towards the centre of the Earth by an invisible force called **gravity**. In some places, the water gets no further than the surface because certain types of rock stop it from draining through. This water forms rivers, lakes and oceans. In other places, different types of rock let the water soak through. All water on Earth eventually settles at the lowest level it can possibly reach.

▲ Waterfalls provide spectacular evidence of how water is pulled down to Earth and always finds its own level. This photograph shows Niagara Falls, which is on the border between the USA and Canada.

Guess the Level

All you need is paper, pencil and scissors.
1. Fold a large sheet of paper in half and then in half again.
2. Draw a bottle shape on one side and cut it out through all four thicknesses of paper.

Fold here

Cut here

3. Put your four 'bottles' in the same positions as the bottles in the illustration below. Draw a line on each one to show where you think the water level would come if the bottles were three-quarters full.

4. Then repeat the experiment with a real bottle of water. (Make sure you hold it over a bath or go outside when you tip it up.) Did you guess the water levels correctly?

The surface of the water in any container is always horizontal – however much you tip the container. Try this for yourself using containers like those in the illustration below.

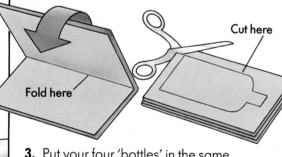

Make Water Flow Upwards

Place one empty bowl on a surface that is lower than the other bowl. Fill the higher bowl with water. Put a finger over one end of the plastic tube and fill it with water. Put the end with your finger over it under the surface of the water in the higher bowl and place the other end in the empty bowl. When you take your finger away, you should see the water flow **up** the tube, out of the higher bowl and down into the other bowl.

How it works
The tube forms a **siphon**, which works because air presses on the surface of the water in the higher bowl and forces water **up** the tube.

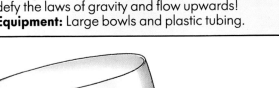

This experiment shows you how to make water defy the laws of gravity and flow upwards!
Equipment: Large bowls and plastic tubing.

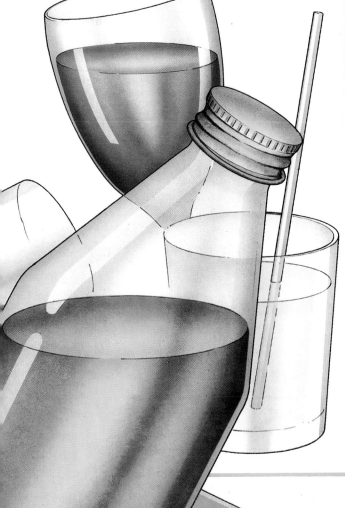

The Impossible Straw

Suck some water up into a straw. Quickly put your finger over the top end and hold out the straw – keep it upright. All the water stays in the straw!

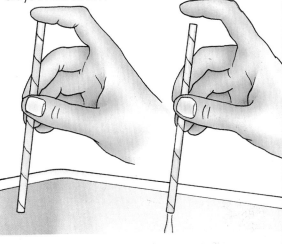

If you take your finger off the end of the straw, the water flows out. This cannot happen unless air can get in at the top to push down on the water and force it out of the straw.

Moving Upwards

On these two pages are some more ways of overcoming the pull of gravity and making water flow upwards. Some of the experiments use air pressure or heat to make the water rise. Others make use of the fact that the water in narrow tubes tends to be pulled upwards by means of a process called **capillary action**.

Colour a Flower

1. Cut about 5 cm (2 inches) off the bottom of a flower stem.
2. Put several drops of colouring in a vase of water.
3. Stand the flower in the water for several hours. Eventually the petals will begin to turn the colour of the water in the vase.

Lift Water in a Glass

Put a glass under the surface of the water in a bowl. Turn it upside down.

Lift it slowly but don't let the rim of the glass come above the surface of the water. What happens?

Then try lifting the glass above the surface of the water. Now what happens?

How it works
Air presses down on the surface of the water and pushes some of the water up into the glass. But when the rim of the glass comes above the surface, the air no longer supports the water and it falls out of the glass.

Underwater Volcano

Equipment: A small bottle, a large glass jar full of water, string, food colouring or ink.

1. Tie the string round the neck of the bottle.
2. Fill the bottle with hot water and add one or two drops of colouring or ink.

3. Carefully lower the small bottle into the large jar. Watch as the coloured water rises upwards, like a volcano.

How it works
The hot water is lighter than the cold water so it rises and floats to the top of the jar. Later, as the hot water cools, it will mix evenly with the cold water and all the water will become the same colour.

Equipment: A freshly cut flower (such as a carnation or daffodil), a vase of water, food colouring or ink.

How it works
The flower 'sucks up' the coloured water through narrow tubes in its stem. The pull of this **capillary action** is enough to overcome the pull of gravity.

More things to try
You can make flowers of more than one colour by splitting the stem in half and standing each half in different coloured water.

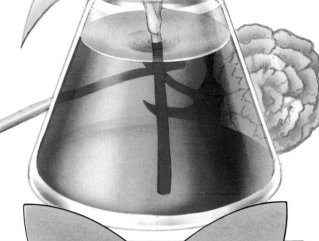

Open a Flower

Equipment: Smooth (but not shiny) paper, pencils, scissors, a bowl of water.

Draw a flower shape like this on your paper and colour it in if you like.

Fold petals like this.

Cut out the flower and fold the petals down flat. When you float the flower on the water, the petals will slowly open as a result of capillary action.

Water gradually rises up through tiny, tube-like holes between the fibres of the paper. The paper swells and the petals open up, just like a real flower.

Flowing Water

The speed at which water flows downwards is controlled by the pull of gravity and the shape of the land. But if water is put under pressure it flows more quickly.

Time how long it takes for the water to reach each one of the levels on your scale.

Make a Water Clock

Thousands of years ago, the Chinese and the Egyptians used flowing water to measure time. You can make a water clock similar to the ones they used.

Equipment: A long ruler, two identical yoghurt cartons or disposable coffee cups, strong, sticky tape, a small nail, modelling clay.
1. Use the nail to make a small hole in the middle of the bottom of one of the containers. Mark a scale on the inside of the other container.
2. Fix the containers to the ruler using sticky tape. Put the container marked with the scale at the bottom. Stand the ruler upright by fixing the end in modelling clay.

3. Cover the hole in the top container with your finger and fill it with water. Then take away your finger and time how long it takes for the water to reach each of the levels in the other container. Can you make a clock that times periods of one minute accurately?

Water and Other Liquids

Investigate how fast water flows compared to other liquids. Prepare two containers in the same way as for the water clock (above). Time how long water takes to drip from one container to another. Then try other liquids, such as treacle, cooking oil or fruit syrup. Which liquid flows fastest?

▼ A model of a Chinese water clock. The wheel moves round each time a bucket fills with water and makes 100 complete turns in 24 hours.

◄ Fire hoses use water that is under high pressure. This makes the water shoot out of the hose in a fast-flowing stream so that a lot of water reaches the fire quickly.

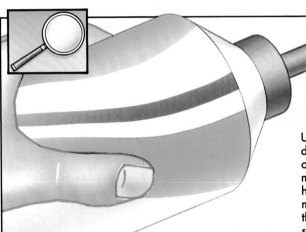

Use a drawing pin or nail to make the holes. They must all be the same size.

Water Power

You can make water flow more quickly by squashing it into a smaller space or by making the water deeper so it puts itself under pressure.

Find an empty washing-up liquid bottle. Take off the cap and fill the bottle with water. Then put the cap back on. Over the bath or out of doors, try squeezing the bottle gently. Then try squeezing it hard. As you press the water into a smaller space, the water will flow faster.

Now empty the bottle again and make three holes in the side. Cover the holes with your fingers and fill the bottle with water. Take away your fingers and see which hole produces the longest jet of water.

How it works
The water at the bottom of the bottle is pushed down by all the water above it so the hole at the bottom produces a long jet of fast flowing water. The other jets are shorter.

25

A Stretchy Skin

Take a good look at raindrops or the drops of water falling from a tap. What shape are the water drops? You should see that the smallest drops are nearly perfect spheres. This is because the surface of the water is held together by a strong force called **surface tension**, which makes the water look as if it has a thin, elastic 'skin' all over it.

Curving Water

Carefully fill a cup or glass with water right to the brim. You will be able to see how surface tension pulls the surface of the water together so it curves above the rim of the container.

Find some dry brushes – a small paint brush and a shaving brush are good ones to try. Look at the shape of the bristles, then dip them in water. You will see that the bristles are pulled together to form a point at the tip of the brushes. Surface tension is strong enough to pull in the bristles and the water.

The Water Walkers

Some insects, such as pond skaters, can walk on water without sinking in. The 'skin' on the surface is strong enough to support them. It bends a little to form small dents around their feet but does not give way. The pond skaters stretch out their long legs to spread their weight over the surface 'skin'.

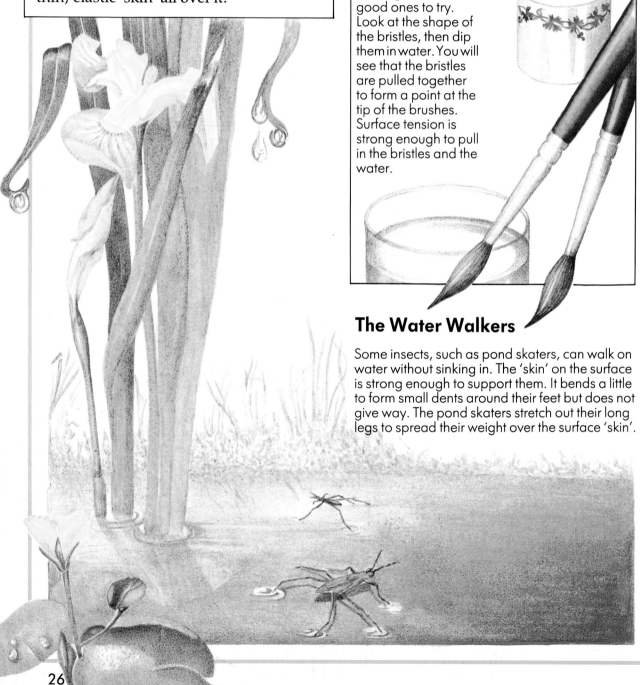

Float the Needle

Can you make metal float on water?

Equipment: A **clean** bowl, a fork, a needle.

1. Fill the bowl with fresh water.

2. Rest the needle across the prongs (tines) of the fork and gently break the surface of the water with the fork. If you are careful, the needle will float off as you take the fork away.

How it works
The fork breaks the 'skin' on the surface of the water but it quickly forms again under the needle. The 'skin' supports the needle and stops it from sinking. If you look closely, you may be able to see the 'skin' bending under the weight of the needle.

Keep the Water Out

Is your handkerchief waterproof? You may be surprised by this trick.

1. Fill a jar with water and soak your handkerchief.

2. Stretch the handkerchief over the mouth of of the jar and hold it in place with string or an elastic band.
3. Turn the jar upside down. Does the water pour out?

How it works
The handkerchief is made of fibres of cloth with tiny holes in between them. Surface tension acts like a 'skin' and stops water pushing down through the holes. Umbrellas stop water getting through for the same reason. Next time you are sheltering under one, think of surface tension.

Pour Water Down a String

Water flowing out of a tap in a steady stream forms a smooth tube. Surface tension keeps the water in this shape. Try pouring water down a string to see this effect for yourself.

Equipment: A small jug, string, an empty container.

1. Tie one end of the string to the handle of the jug. Fill the jug with water.
2. Pass the string over the lip of the jug and hold the free end against the inside of the container.
3. Separate the jug and the container so the string is pulled tight.
4. Hold the jug right above the container and pour slowly and carefully. The water should flow down the string into the container.
5. After the flow has started, move the jug down so it is at an angle. Surface tension should hold the water close to the string so it flows along it.

Tie string to handle of jug.

Tie Water in Knots

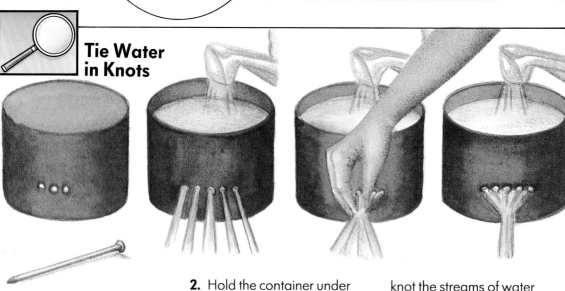

1. Use a nail to make 5 even holes near the bottom of a plastic container. The holes should be about 0.5 cm (¼ inch) apart.

2. Hold the container under a tap in a sink and fill it with water. You will see 5 streams of water coming out.

3. Pinch the 5 streams of water together with your fingers. You should be able to

knot the streams of water together using the pull of surface tension.

4. If you brush your hand across the holes, you should be able to separate the streams of water again.

Break the Tension

Surface tension can cause unexpected things to happen. It can support objects that look as if they should sink.

Equipment: A bowl of water, a plastic basket (similar to the one in the illustration below).

1. Fill the bowl with water and gently lower the basket on to the surface. The basket should float – even though it is full of holes!

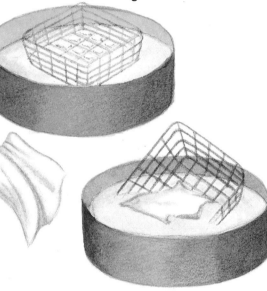

2. Now take a small piece of tissue and drop it lightly into the basket. The tissue slowly soaks up water and the basket should suddenly sink.

How it works
The basket floats because surface tension acts like a 'skin' and stops water pushing up through the holes. But when the tissue soaks up water, it breaks the 'skin' and the surface of the water cannot support the basket.

Stretching the Skin

What happens when the pull of surface tension is weakened? How stretchy is water's 'skin'?

1. Choose a large, clean plate and rinse it well.
2. Fill the plate with water and wait until the surface is smooth and still. Then sprinkle talcum powder over the surface.

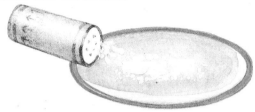

3. Wet one finger and rub it over a piece of soap. Then dip your finger in the water at one side of the plate. All the talcum will be drawn immediately to the other side of the plate.

How it works
Soap weakens the pull of surface tension in the water around your finger. The pull from the opposite side of the plate is stronger and the talcum powder is drawn over there.

Soap Power

Soap weakens the surface tension that makes the 'skin' form on the surface of water. This stretches the 'skin' and makes it possible to blow bubbles. It also makes enough pulling power to drive small boats. On these two pages are some tricks to try and things to make using this soap power.

Soap Boats

Equipment: Card or wood, scissors, small pieces of soap, bowl of water.

1. Make a boat shape out of card or wood and cut a notch in the middle at the back. Fix a tiny piece of soap in the notch.

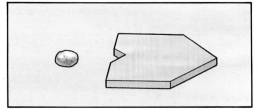

2. Fill a **clean** bowl or wash basin with water and let the water settle. Put your boat on the water and watch it move.

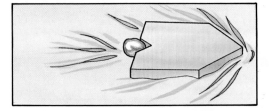

How it works
The soap weakens the surface tension behind the boat and it is pulled forward by the stronger surface tension in front.

More things to try
● Make the notch for the soap to one side of the back of the boat – what happens?
● Try adding a rudder of paperclips to steer the boat.

Magic Matchsticks

Equipment: Matches, bowl of **clean** water, soap, lump of sugar.

1. Carefully lay the matches on the surface of the water.

2. Dip the sugar lump in the middle of the bowl. The matches should move towards the sugar.

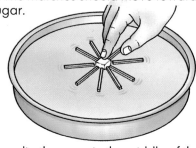

3. Now dip the soap in the middle of the bowl. The matches should move away from the soap.

How it works
When you put the sugar lump in the middle of the bowl, it absorbs some of the water. A small current of water flows towards the sugar and pulls the matches with it. But when you hold the soap in the middle of the bowl, the stronger surface tension around the edge of the bowl pulls the matches outwards.

Blowing Bubbles

You can see just how stretchy the 'skin' on the surface of water can be by blowing bubbles. You can buy bubble mixtures with a wand or you can make your own.

Bubble Recipe
Put three or four tablespoons of soap powder or soap flakes into four cups of hot water. Let the mixture stand for three days and then stir in a large spoonful of sugar. This gives extra strong bubbles.

Bubble Blowers
You can make a bubble blower by bending a piece of fuse wire (or other thin wire) into a circle. Dip your bubble blower into the soap mixture and blow through it very gently. The 'skin' will stretch and eventually a bubble will break free.

Try to find out ...
- Are the bubbles all the same shape?
- How big can the bubbles be?
- How long do they last?
- What makes them pop?

Crystal Bubbles

Take your bubble blower and soap mixture outside when it is very cold and there is no wind. Use a round bubble blower and gently blow a large bubble. Do not let the bubble blow away and hold it still. If it is very cold, the thin bubble should begin to freeze as you watch. You should be able to see tiny crystals forming over the surface of the bubble until it freezes completely. Then you will have a very thin ice crystal ball.

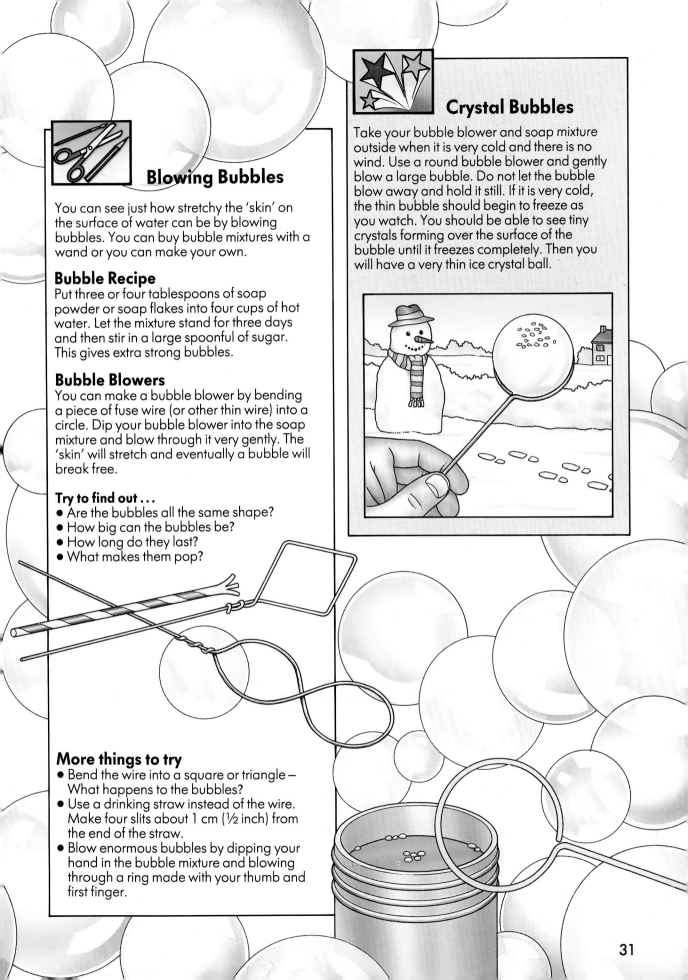

More things to try
- Bend the wire into a square or triangle – What happens to the bubbles?
- Use a drinking straw instead of the wire. Make four slits about 1 cm (½ inch) from the end of the straw.
- Blow enormous bubbles by dipping your hand in the bubble mixture and blowing through a ring made with your thumb and first finger.

Floating and Sinking

Why do some objects float and others sink? Do large objects float more easily than small ones? Does the shape of an object make any difference? Try these experiments to find out.

Will it Float on Water?

Choose several solid objects – make sure they are not hollow. Guess which ones will float and then test them in a bowl of water or in the bath.

Objects to test: A stone, an orange, an apple, a screw, pieces of wood, an egg, coins, polystyrene, pumice stone, candle, seeds, erasers.

How it works

Water tries to support solid objects. If the objects are heavy for their size, they will sink; if they are light for their size, they will float. An object that is heavy for its size is said to have a high **density**. An empty lift has a low density but as it begins to fill with people, its density increases. Its size stays the same, however. This is why objects that are the same size can have different densities. A brick is more dense than a piece of wood of the same size because the stony particles that make up the brick are heavy and packed more tightly together than the fibres in the block of wood.

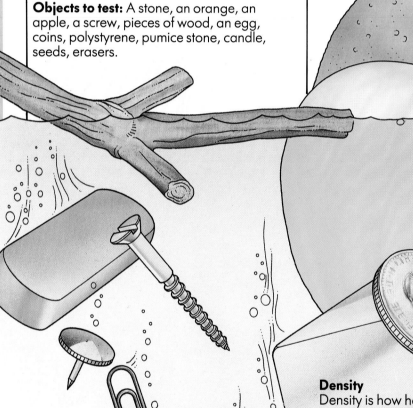

Density

Density is how heavy something is compared to its volume. You can work out the density of an object by dividing its weight by its volume. One cubic centimetre of water weighs one gram, so water has a density of one. If an object has a density greater than one, it will sink in water. If an object has a density of less than one, it will float on water.

Does Wood Float?

When you investigated floating and sinking, you probably found that pieces of wood float easily. But did you know that some types of wood sink in water? Pieces of cork (the bark of cork trees) and maple float easily but mahogany is only just supported by water. Ebony (the hard, black wood sometimes used to make piano keys) does not float at all because it is more dense than water.

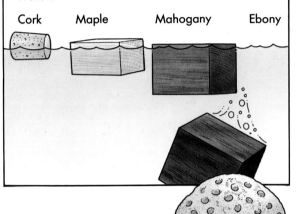

Cork   Maple   Mahogany   Ebony

More things to try

Now that you have tested solid floaters and sinkers, mould a ball of modelling clay into different shapes and see if they float. Use the same amount of clay each time. Here are a few shapes to try:

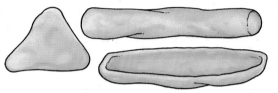

A solid ball of modelling clay will sink straight to the bottom. But if you make it into a boat shape with high sides, it will float. So the shape of floaters and sinkers **is** important. Turn over to find out more . . .

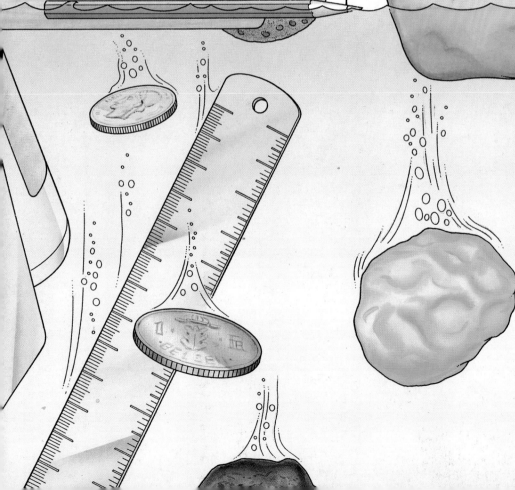

Pushing Water Out of the Way

Both the density (p.32–33) and the shape of an object affect whether it will float or sink in water. The shape of an object controls the amount of water that it pushes out of the way or '**displaces**'. If the amount of water that is displaced weighs more than the object, it will float. If the displaced water weighs less than the object, it will sink.

▶ A large ship floats because it displaces a lot of water. Even though the ship is heavy, it still weighs less than the amount of water it displaces.

Experiment With Size and Shape

Try lifting something heavy (such as a full tin) underwater and then lift the same object in air. You will find that things are much lighter and easier to lift under the water. This is because the water pushes up under the objects and tries to support them. But how much less do they weigh? Objects that are completely underwater lose the same weight as the weight of water they displace.

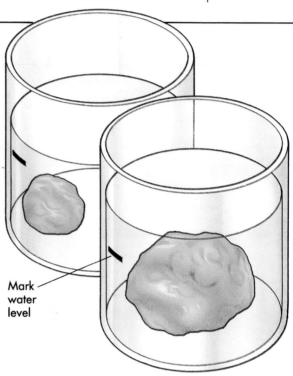

Mark water level

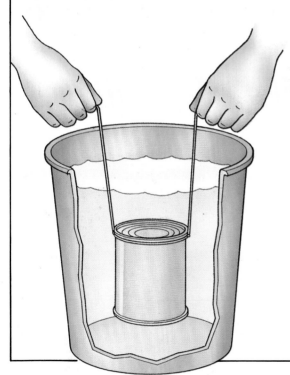

The amount of water that an object pushes out of the way or 'displaces' depends partly on its size. Large objects displace more water.

Fill a jar with water and mark the level. Drop in a ball of modelling clay and see how the level rises. Then try a much larger ball and see how much more the level rises.

Ships may sink if they are overloaded so all ships have a mark like this on the side. It tells the captain how low the ship can float in the water without sinking.

This mark is called the Plimsoll line after its inventor, Samuel Plimsoll.

Loading the Boat

Make a boat out of modelling clay or paper or use a toy boat. Float the boat in the water and mark the water level on the side. Load your boat with small items, such as paper clips. Add a few at a time and watch your boat float lower and lower in the water. How much cargo will your boat carry before it sinks? This is how the Plimsoll line works (see above).

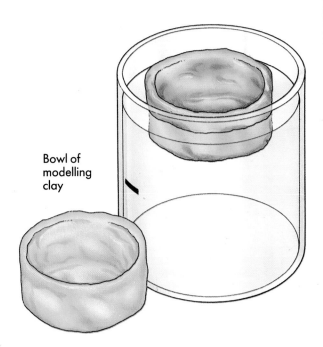

Bowl of modelling clay

As well as size, the amount of water displaced by an object has a lot to do with its shape.

Change the shape of your piece of modelling clay to make a bowl. When you float the bowl in the jar, you will see that far more water is pushed out of the way and the level of water in the jar will be higher than before. Both the bowl and the air inside it push water out of the way.

35

Make a Pen-top Diver

This fascinating toy works in a similar way to a submarine by displacing water to make it dive and re-surface.

Equipment: A tall bottle, a pen-top, modelling clay or paperclips, string or an elastic band and a thin rubber sheet.

1. Fill the bottle to the brim with water. Add the modelling clay or paperclips to make the pen-top heavier until it **just** floats and is on the point of sinking. (You can fix the paperclips with fine thread or make a hole in the pen-top to loop them through.) Take plenty of time to get this right.

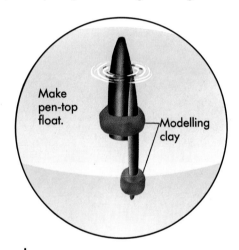

Make pen-top float.

Modelling clay

How it works
Plastic is only a little heavier than water. A bubble of air is trapped inside the pen-top and this is enough to make it float. When you press down on the rubber lid, you squeeze the tiny air bubble into a smaller space so more water can get inside the pen-top. This make the pen-top heavier so it sinks. When you stop pressing, the air can expand and push out the extra water so the pen-top rises.

More things to try
Make another sort of diver using orange peel – you could cut out a boat shape from the peel. The peel contains tiny bubbles of air so it will sink and rise in the same way as the pen-top. You will find it always floats with the orange side down because the orange part of the peel is heavier.

How a Submarine Works

Submarines use the principle of displacement to enable them to dive and come up to the surface again. At the surface, submarines float in the same way as ordinary ships. But they have special tanks inside them that can be filled with air or water to change the weight of the submarine. You can see how this works for yourself if you float a bottle full of air and gradually allow it to fill with water.

2. Stretch the sheet of rubber over the mouth of the bottle and hold it in place with string or the elastic band. Press down on the rubber with the palm of your hand and your 'diver' will go down! When you take your hand away, it will rise again.

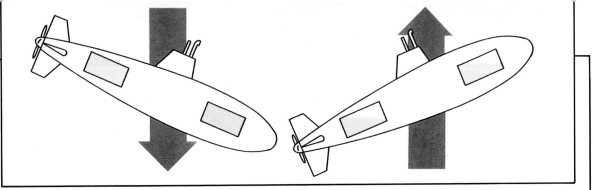

When the submarine is ready to dive, the tanks are flooded with sea water. This makes the submarine heavier than the water it displaces, so it sinks.

To return to the surface, compressed air is pumped into the tanks. This forces out the sea water and makes the submarine lighter than the water it displaces, so it floats again.

Bouncing Moth Balls

1. Fill the glass jar with water. Stir in about ⅓ cup of vinegar and two teaspoons of bicarbonate of soda. Stir slowly and carefully so the mixture does not froth up too much.

2. Drop a few moth balls into the fizzy liquid. At first they will sink to the bottom but after a little while each one will rise to the surface again. But they will not stay there! They will keep sinking to the bottom and bouncing up again for several hours.

How it works
The bubbles are a gas called carbon dioxide, which is formed when the vinegar and bicarbonate of soda join together in a chemical reaction. (This is the same gas that makes the bubbles in fizzy drinks.) If you look carefully at the moth balls, you will see that they collect bubbles when they are on the bottom. The bubbles are lighter than water and they lift the moth balls up to the surface. But lots of the bubbles escape into the air and the moth balls become too heavy for the few remaining bubbles to support them – so they sink again. On the bottom, they soon collect more bubbles and bounce up again.

Hint
If the moth balls are too smooth, the bubbles cannot hold on, so the trick will not work. Rub the moth balls with sandpaper to make the surface rough.

Liquid Layers

It is not only solid things that either float or sink in water. Different liquids also have different **densities** (see pages 32–33), which means that some are heavier than others. If a liquid does not mix with water, it is possible to find out if it is more or less dense than water.

▶ This boat is spraying an oil slick, which is floating on the surface of the sea. The spray makes the oil sink to the bottom so it does not float towards land and pollute the beaches.

Find the Density

Equipment: Water, syrup, cooking oil (about a cup of each), a tall glass jar, a jug.

Pour the liquids carefully into the glass jar one after the other. You will see that they separate into three layers – the syrup sinks below the water and the oil floats on top.
Which liquid has the highest density?

Try floating some objects on your liquid layers. Things you might try include: a piece of candle, a cork, a slice of apple, a grape, a metal object.

Do they float? Which layer do they float on? You could make a chart of your results in a notebook.

Pour the liquids over a spoon so they do not mix.

Oil

Water

Syrup

The Magic Egg Trick

Salt water is more dense than fresh water, which is why it is easier to float in the sea. You can use this scientific fact to perform a magic trick with an egg.

Equipment: Two glasses, salt, two eggs.

Salt water   Fresh water

Mix plenty of salt (about 10 heaped teaspoons) into half a glass of water. Fill the second glass half full of fresh water. Try floating an egg in each glass. You will find that the egg will float in the salt water because it is **less** dense than salt water. But the egg will sink in the fresh water because it is **more** dense than fresh water.

Now try this magic trick.
Fill one glass half full of fresh water and one half full of very salty water, as before. Then, very carefully, pour the fresh water into the salt water. Don't let the liquids mix. Gently lower the egg into the water. It should float on the salt water and look as if it is suspended in the middle of the glass by magic!

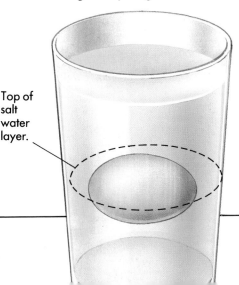

Top of salt water layer.

Water Mixtures

If you mix sugar into tea, it disappears and the tea tastes sweet. This is called **dissolving** and the experiments on these two pages will help you to investigate this process. On pages 42 and 43 you can find out how the dissolved substances can be separated from the water again.

Salt-in-Water Trick

Take a glass full of water and an egg cup full of salt. Do you think you can dissolve all the salt in the water without making the glass overflow?

Try it and see. Sprinkle the salt gently on to the water and use a thin wire to stir it in. When substances dissolve, they do not take up extra space.

Mixing Oil and Water

Water and oil do not mix. Birds keep their feathers waterproof by spreading oil from a special gland onto their feathers. Try mixing oil and water for yourself and see what happens.

1. Put a little cooking oil and water in a jar. Fix the lid on firmly and shake the jar hard. When you put the jar down, the oil and water will separate into two layers.

2. Now add a few drops of washing-up liquid and shake the jar again. This will produce a cloudy mixture.

How it works
The soap in the washing-up liquid breaks up the oil into small drops, which hang in the water and make it look cloudy. This is how washing-up liquid helps to remove grease from plates and saucepans.

Dissolving Tests

Many substances dissolve in water but some do not. Investigate some of these: salt, fine sand, tea leaves, washing soda, bicarbonate of soda, rice, jelly. Stir a small amount of each substance into a jar of water and make a note of what happens. Does it make a difference if the water is warm ?

Make Your Own Stalactites

Stalactites and stalagmites are columns of stone, which form in underground caves. They are made from minerals dissolved in the rainwater that drips slowly from the roofs and walls of caves. As it drips, the water evaporates (see p. 12–13) and leaves the dissolved minerals behind.

Equipment: Two glass jars, woollen thread, washing soda.
1. Fill the two jars with very warm water. Dissolve as much washing soda in each one as you can.

2. Place the two jars in a warm place and put a saucer between them. Twist several strands of woollen thread together. Dip one end of the thread in each jar and let it hang down in the middle. The two solutions should creep along the thread until they reach the middle and then drip onto the saucer.

3. Leave the jars in place for several days and you will see tiny stalactites and stalagmites forming in the centre of the wool. As the water evaporates, a column of crystals forms.

▼ Stalagtites hang down from the roof of a cave; stalagmites grow up from the cave floor.

Mixing Gases With Water

- Fizzy drinks contain a gas called carbon dioxide dissolved in them. When you open a can or bottle of fizzy drink, the fizz you can hear and feel is bubbles of the gas escaping.
- Air dissolves in water too. Pumps connected to fish tanks force air into the water so the fishes can breathe.
- Hot water holds less dissolved gas than cold water. As you heat water, the bubbles you can see are bubbles of air escaping into the atmosphere.

How to Make Fresh Water

Sea water is too salty for drinking. But it is possible to remove the salts dissolved in it and make it fit to drink. This is carried out on a large scale at desalination plants, although it is an expensive process. Sea water is heated until it evaporates and the vapour is condensed back to liquid water by passing it over hundreds of pipes that contain cold water. Try making a small amount of fresh water for yourself to see how it is done.

Ask an adult to help you. Take care with hot pans and liquids and don't forget to turn off the heat when you have finished.

Equipment: Salt, water, a clean cup, oven gloves, a saucepan with a lid.

How it works
As the water boils, it evaporates and turns to vapour, which condenses on the cool lid to form drops of liquid water (see pages 14–15). The salt cannot do this and stays behind in the saucepan. So the water you collect from the saucepan lid should not taste salty.

Salt

Wait until water is cool before you taste it.

1. Pour water into the saucepan until it is about 5–8 cm (2–3 inches) deep. Mix in lots of salt. Taste it – Ugh!

2. Heat the water until it boils and keep it simmering gently. Put the lid on the saucepan.

3. Use the oven gloves to lift off the lid. Tip the drops of water into the cup. Replace the lid and do this again until you have enough to taste.

Cleaning Water

Most of the water people use for drinking, washing and cooking comes from rivers, lakes or wells. In the richer countries of the world, water is cleaned before and after it is used. The water is first pumped to reservoirs where it is stored until it is needed. Then it travels to a water treatment works where dirt is removed and chlorine is added to kill any harmful germs in the water (see photo). After this clean water has been used by people, the dirty water is carried away in the sewers to a sewage works. There any dirt is removed and special bacteria are added to eat up any harmful germs. The clean water is returned to the rivers again.

Remove the Mud

Here is another way to clean water by removing some of the substances it contains. In this case, the substance to be removed (mud) is not dissolved in the water but floats throughout the water. All you need are two containers and a handkerchief or small towel. Fill one container with muddy water and put it higher than the other container. Place one end of the handkerchief or towel into the muddy water and let the other end hang down into the other bowl.

How it works

The water rises up the narrow air spaces in the cloth by **capillary action** (see pages 22–23) and then trickles slowly down the cloth into the lower container. Mud particles cannot do this and are left behind.

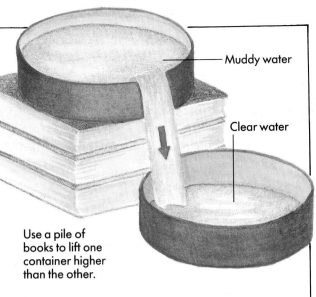

Muddy water

Clear water

Use a pile of books to lift one container higher than the other.

Warning:
Do not drink the water; it may contain harmful germs.

How to Filter Water

This experiment will help you to understand one of the stages in cleaning water at a water treatment works.

Equipment: Muddy water, a plastic bottle, coffee filter paper, some sand, barbecue charcoal (crushed to a powder).

1. Cut the top off the bottle about 8–10 cm (3–4 inches) down from the lid.
2. Turn the top upside down and rest it in the remainder of the bottle. Put in a coffee filter and a layer of wet sand. Then pour some muddy water onto the sand. You will see that it looks a little cleaner as it drips through the filter.
3. You could try to improve your filter by putting a layer of **powdered** charcoal above the sand and then adding another layer of sand above the charcoal. Particles of dirt will be trapped in the layers and this helps to clean the water. The fine particles in the powdered charcoal trap more dirt than the larger grains of sand.

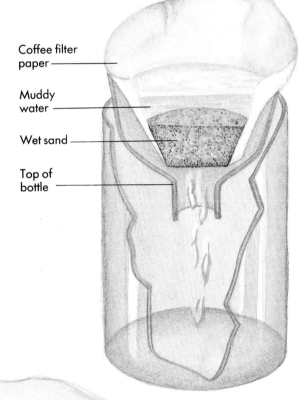

Coffee filter paper

Muddy water

Wet sand

Top of bottle

Warning
Do not drink the water; it may contain harmful germs.

Powdered charcoal

Filter paper

Water for Life

Did you know that at least 65 per cent of your body is water? Or that 95 per cent of a jellyfish is made up of water? All living things have a high percentage of water in their bodies and need water to survive. Many plants and animals spend their whole lives in water. Others survive with very little water.

► In some countries, people have to walk a long way every day to collect water from a well. This well is in an African country called Malawi.

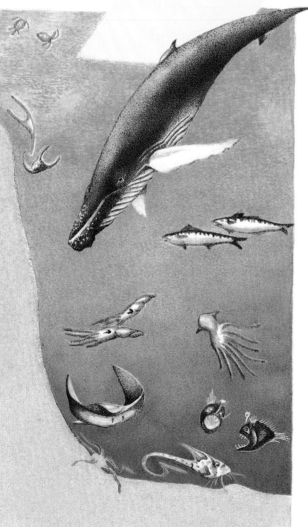

The Ocean Dwellers

Plants and animals that live in the oceans obtain all the air and food they need from the water around them. Some animals hunt for food; others stay put and wait for it to drift past. Microscopic animals floating in the water provide a source of food for many animals, including some of the great whales. These whales have bony plates (called baleen plates) with fringes on the end in their mouths. The fringe strains tiny animals from the sea water. At the bottom of the oceans, it is very cold and dark and no plants can survive. Many of the animals feed on the dead bodies of plants and animals, which drift down from the surface.

Water supports the bodies of plants and animals. You can see this if you compare the appearance of seaweed under the water and in the air.

In air

In water

Water From the Desert

This experiment shows you how to collect water from sand that seems too dry to contain any water at all. You can try it in a sand pit or at the seaside.

Dig a hole about 60 cm (2 feet) deep and put a cup in the centre. Cover the hole with a sheet of plastic so that it dips down in the middle. Weigh the sheet down with a stone and hold the edges down firmly with stones and sand. As the Sun shines, drops of water will slowly form underneath the plastic sheet and run down into the cup.

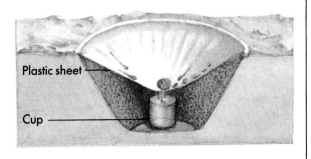

Plastic sheet

Cup

How it works
The heat of the Sun warms the sand under the plastic sheet and some of the moisture in the sand evaporates and then condenses on the plastic (see pages 14–15).

Desert Survival

Plants and animals that live in the desert cope with the lack of water in a variety of ways. Some plants, such as cacti, store water in their stems. Others, including mesquite trees, have deep roots to reach water deep underground. Many plants survive the dry conditions as seeds buried in the desert sand and flower only after a rainstorm. Many desert animals spend the day in underground burrows or rest in the shade. They come out to search for food and water at night, when it is cooler. Some desert animals have to get most of their water from the food they eat.

▲ Look out for water wheels when you are in the countryside. See if you can work out how the water makes the wheel turn round and try to find out what the water power was used for. This water wheel is in the Black Forest region of Germany.

Water Power

The power of moving water has been used for hundreds of years as a source of energy. Water-mills on the banks of fast-flowing rivers used water power to turn stones, which ground wheat into flour. Today, hydro-electric power stations all over the world use the energy of flowing water to produce electricity. The energy of tides and waves can also be used to produce electricity.

Energy From the Tides

A dam on the estuary of the River Rance in Brittany, France uses the power of the tides to make electricity. The water trapped by the dam is released through 24 special turbines, which can spin in either direction. This means that electricity can be generated both as the tide comes in and as it goes out.

Hydro-Electric Power

Hydro-electric power stations use the power of falling water to produce electricity. The water may come from natural waterfalls, such as Niagara Falls, or from the water held back by artificial dams. The water rushes over large wheels called turbines and makes them turn. This drives machines called generators, which produce electricity. You can see how this works in the diagram below.

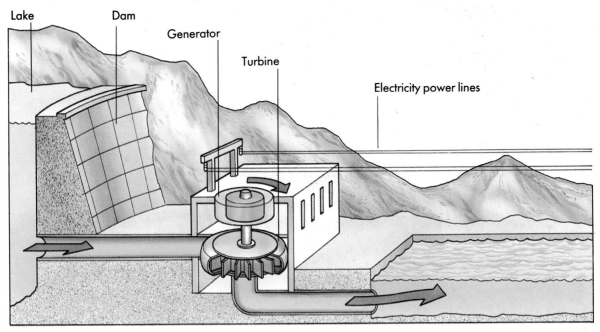

Lake   Dam   Generator   Turbine   Electricity power lines

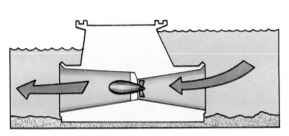

As the tide rises, water flows in from the sea and turns the turbines as it passes into the estuary.

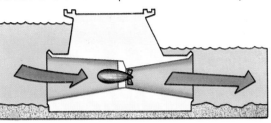

As the tide falls, the water turns the turbines in the opposite direction as it flows back out to sea.

Wave Energy

The movement of the waves can also be used to make electricity. One experimental machine for harnessing wave energy is called the 'nodding boom' or 'duck'. The waves make the 'beak' of each 'duck' nod up and down. This energy is used to produce electricity in small generators inside the 'ducks' themselves.

Water Quiz

True or False?

1. Clouds are made of water.

2. Drops of water are round because surface tension holds them in this shape.

3. Salt makes snow melt.

4. Snowflakes always have 8 sides.

Spot the Mistakes

5. What is wrong with these pictures?

Talcum powder

Syrup

Oil

Water

Washing-up liquid

6. Which one of these substances will make oil and water mix together?

7. Which of these objects will float in water?

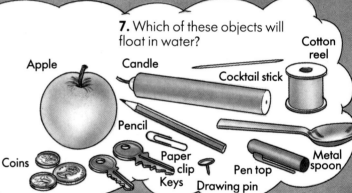

Apple

Candle

Cotton reel

Cocktail stick

Pencil

Paper clip

Pen top

Metal spoon

Coins

Keys

Drawing pin

Answers

1. True. Clouds are made of tiny drops of water, which form when water vapour condenses in cold air. Some clouds contain ice crystals (page 15).

2. True. Surface tension makes water look as if it has a thin, elastic 'skin', and holds it together (page 26).

3. True. This is because salt water freezes at a lower temperature than ordinary water. Salt will turn snow back into liquid unless it is very, very cold (page 19).

4. False. Snowflakes always have 6 sides (page 16).

5. Left: Ice is less dense than water so the ice cubes should be floating (page 16).
Right: The water in all the containers should be horizontal (pages 20-21).

6. Washing-up liquid. The soap in the washing-up liquid breaks up the oil into small drops, which can mix with the water more easily (page 40).

7. Float: Apple, Candle, Cotton reel, Cocktail stick, Pencil, Pen top.
They float because they are less dense than water (pages 32-33).
Sink: Keys, Paper clip, Metal spoon, Coins, Drawing pin.

AIR

This section of the book will help you to investigate air. Think about air when you watch planes or helicopters fly or when the weather is stormy.

There are six main topics in this section:

- Air and weight
- Warm air
- Air pressure
- Moving air and compressed air
- Air and the weather
- Air and burning; life; sound

Use the symbols below to help you identify the three kinds of practical activities in this book.

EXPERIMENTS

TRICKS

THINGS TO MAKE

Introduction

You breathe in air every day of your life and the oxygen in the air keeps you alive but most of the time you hardly notice the air all around you. One of the few times you can see air is when bubbles of air are produced underwater. But it is much easier to see the effect of air on your surroundings.

When air is heated, it becomes lighter and rises. Birds and gliders use rising currents of warm air to float in the sky. When air moves, it has enough power to push sailing boats along and drive windmills. When air is squashed (compressed) into a small space it has great strength. The compressed air in a car tyre supports the weight of the vehicle and compressed air also helps a helicopter to rise up into the air.

As you carry out the experiments in this book you will come to understand the different characteristics of air. This will help you to answer the questions on these two pages and explain how air influences the way in which things happen in the world around you.

▲ During a storm, why do you see the lightning before you hear the thunder? (page 87)

▼ How does an aircraft take off and stay up in the air? (pages 76–77)

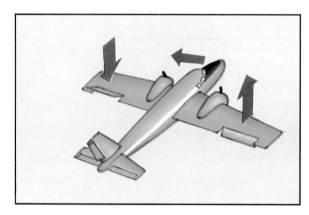

◀ Why does a parachute fall down to Earth slowly? (page 74)

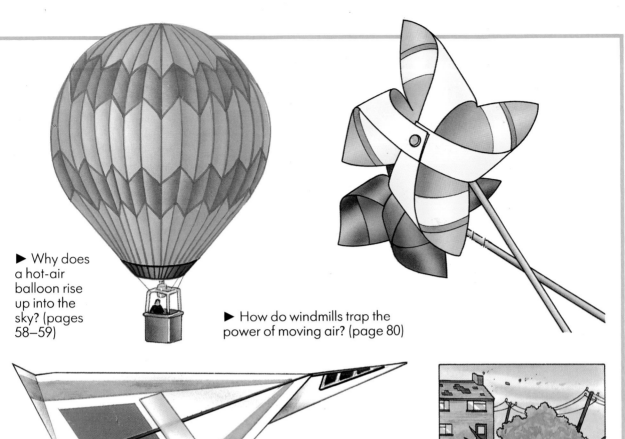

► Why does a hot-air balloon rise up into the sky? (pages 58–59)

► How do windmills trap the power of moving air? (page 80)

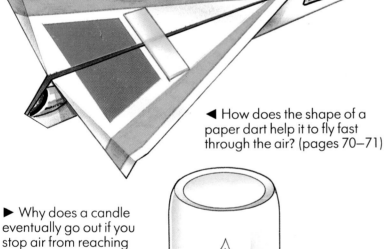

◄ How does the shape of a paper dart help it to fly fast through the air? (pages 70–71)

▲ How fast can the wind travel? What damage can a hurricane cause? (pages 78–79)

► Why does a candle eventually go out if you stop air from reaching it? (page 82)

▼ How does a helicopter take off straight up into the air? (pages 72–73)

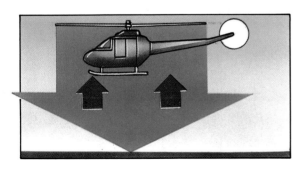

► How does double glazing help to keep a house warm? (page 61)

Where is Air?

Air is all around you but it is difficult to investigate because you cannot see, taste or touch it. Air does not smell either, although it is possible to detect the scent of flowers, cooking, petrol fumes and other substances, which are carried by the air. You can feel air when it moves however, and see the effect it has on other things. It makes grass or trees sway and bend, it pushes litter along the street and makes clouds move.

Divers strap tanks of air on their backs so they can breathe underwater. When they breathe out, bubbles of used air escape into the water. This is an archaeologist on an underwater dig.

Looking for Air

As well as being all around us, air fills tiny spaces in all sorts of things. You can see this air by putting objects underwater and watching for bubbles of air to escape.

1. Push a bottle underwater and let it fill up. As water rushes in, bubbles of air rush out.

2. Now try a clay flower pot and then a small amount of soil. How much air do they contain?

3. Investigate water itself next. Place a glass of water in a warm place for about an hour. You will see small bubbles of air rising in the water or collecting on the sides of the glass. As the water gets warmer, some of the bubbles escape into the air. When water boils, a lot of large bubbles of air escape. This shows that there is air in water itself.

Fill a Glass With Air

1. Turn one of the glasses upside down. Keep it straight and push it under the water. You will see that it stays full of air.
2. Hold the glass of air under the water with one hand and put the second glass under the water with the other hand. Turn the second glass on its side as you lower it so it fills with water.
3. Move the two glasses together and tilt the first glass so that bubbles of air begin to rise into the second glass.

Equipment: Two clear glasses , a large bowl of water.

How it works
Water in the second glass is driven out by air rising from the first glass. The first glass fills with water, which replaces the lost air.

Air Needs Space

Equipment: A clear plastic bottle, a funnel, modelling clay, knitting needle or pencil.

Seal with modelling clay.

Hole in modelling clay.

Air fills spaces that look empty. Try an experiment to test this.
1. Put the funnel in the neck of the bottle and seal up the gap using modelling clay.
2. Pour some water into the funnel. You may be surprised to see that the water does not flow into the bottle.
3. Use the knitting needle or pencil to make a small hole in the modelling clay. What happens?

How it works
The bottle was full of air but the modelling clay stopped the air escaping. When you made a hole in the clay, the air was able to get out of the bottle as water rushed in to fill the space. This can also happen in reverse. You cannot pour liquid from a can if there is only one small hole in it. As you tip the can, the liquid inside seals the hole and air cannot get inside to replace the liquid. If you make another hole in the can, air can get in as the liquid flows out.

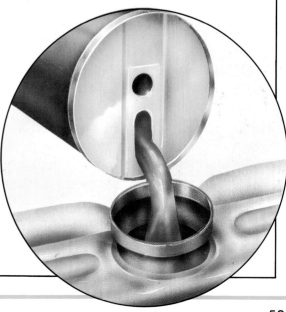

As Light as Air

Air takes up space all around us but how much does it weigh? Scientists use complex and delicate instruments to measure the weight of very light substances. You can weigh air by making a simple balance like the one in the diagram below.

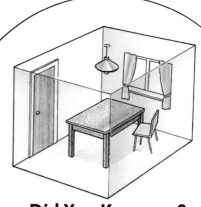

Did You Know . . . ?

The air in a large room in your house weighs about as much as a person (72 kilograms or 11 stone).

Weighing Air

1. Mark the middle of your stick.
2. Rest the pencil between the tins and place the middle of the stick across the pencil so the stick is level.
3. Use a small piece of sticky tape to fix a balloon on to each end of the stick. Check that the stick remains level – this means that the balloons weigh the same.
4. Unstick one of the balloons and blow as much air into it as you can.
5. Fix it back on to the end of the stick. Does the stick still balance?

Equipment: Two identical balloons, string, a long stick, sticky tape, two tins, a pencil with flat sides.

How it works

When you stick the full balloon back on, it makes the stick dip down. This shows it is heavier than the empty balloon and the air that you blew into the balloon does weigh something.

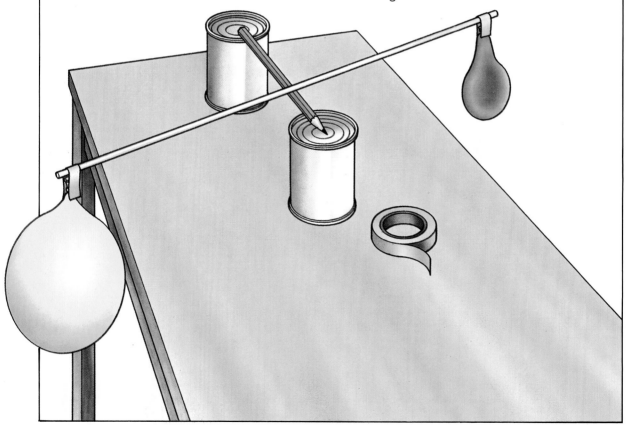

Keep the Tissue Dry

Can you put a paper tissue in water without getting it wet? All you need is a bowl of water, a small glass and a paper tissue.

Screw the paper tissue into a ball and push it into the glass. Turn the glass upside down and place it under the water in the bowl. You should find that water does not enter the glass and the tissue stays dry!

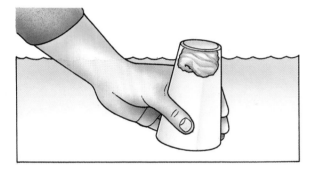

How it works
Water cannot get into the glass because it is full of air. And air cannot get out because it is lighter than water, so the tissue does not get wet.

Make a Submarine

Here is a way of making a toy submarine that goes up and down on 'air power'.
Equipment: A plastic bottle with a narrow neck, modelling clay, a piece of plastic tubing, coins, sticky tape.

1. Cut two or three small holes in the side of the bottle. Use the sticky tape to fix three or four coins on to the same side of the bottle. (These will act as weights and help the submarine to sink.)
2. Put the plastic tubing in the neck of the bottle and seal the neck with modelling clay.
3. Lower the submarine into the bowl of water and let it fill with water.
4. Blow through the tube to force air into the submarine. As you blow, water will be forced out of the holes in the bottom.
5. As the submarine begins to fill with air, it will slowly rise to the surface. You can make it rise and sink by changing the amount of air inside it.

How it works
Air weighs less than water. (You could test this on the balance on the previous page.) When you fill the submarine with air, it becomes lighter than the water and rises to the surface.

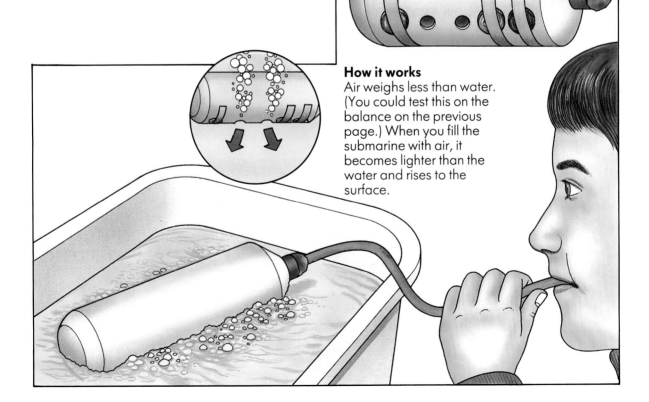

A Lot of Hot Air

Warm air is lighter than cold air so air rises as it gets warm and cold air moves in to take its place. This causes currents of air to move around inside buildings and out of doors as well. Birds float upwards on rising currents of hot air and gliders stay up in the air in the same way.

Warm Air Rises

In the rooms in a house, cold air gets into the room through windows and under the doors. It is warmed by fires or radiators, becomes lighter and rises to the ceiling. When this happens, cooler air moves in to take its place. This movement of air around a room is called a **convection current**. Warm air may escape from a room through the doors and windows again. You can find out more about how to stop the air escaping and keep rooms warm on pages 60–61.

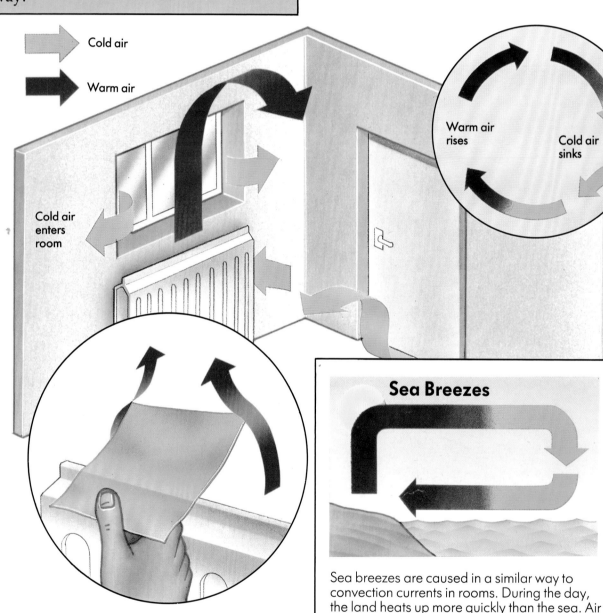

Cold air

Warm air

Cold air enters room

Warm air rises

Cold air sinks

Sea Breezes

Sea breezes are caused in a similar way to convection currents in rooms. During the day, the land heats up more quickly than the sea. Air over the land becomes warmer and rises. Cooler air from the sea moves in to take its place.

You can see the current of warm air rising if you hold a piece of tissue paper over a radiator. The warm air will push the tissue upwards.

Floating on Air

Gliders have to be towed up into the sky but once they are high enough, they can use rising currents of warm air to stay up in the air. These currents of warm air are called **thermals**. At the top of one thermal the pilot has to find and reach another thermal before the glider drops too far. A glider can travel hundreds of kilometres on a warm day.

Make a Spinning Snake

Equipment: A square of paper, pencil, scissors, thread.

This spinning snake is a good way to observe rising air and have some fun. Draw a spiral like this on the square of paper. Decorate the snake and then carefully cut along the line of the spiral. Hang the snake above a radiator using the piece of thread and watch it spin as the warm air rises.

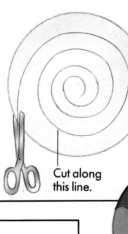

Cut along this line.

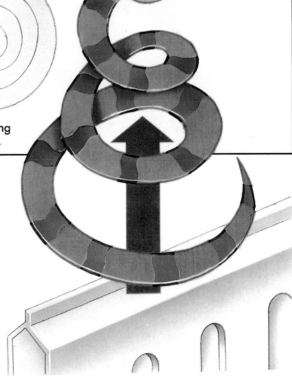

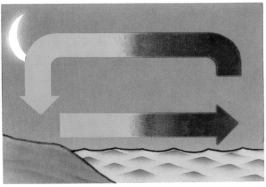

At night, the land cools down more quickly than the sea, so the sea is warmer than the land. A convection current is formed in the opposite direction to the daytime current. Warm air over the sea rises and cool air from the land moves in to take its place.

More things to try
- To keep your snake spinning longer, fix it on the tip of a pencil by making a small hole in the head end. Keep the pencil upright by placing the unsharpened end in some modelling clay or pushing it inside a cotton reel.
- Try making a 'sparkling' snake using tin foil.

Investigating Hot Air

Equipment: A plastic bottle, a balloon, a deep bowl, hot water, ice.

Air takes up space but did you know that hot air takes up more space than cold air? Prove it for yourself in this experiment.

Hot water

Ice

1. Fit the balloon over the mouth of the bottle.
2. Stand the bottle in the bowl and fill the bowl with hot water. After a few minutes you will see the balloon start to inflate.
3. Tip away the water and fill the bowl with ice. What happens?

How it works
When the air is warmed by the hot water, it expands and needs more space so it stretches out the balloon. When the air is cooled by the ice, it contracts and needs less space so the balloon goes down.

Balloon Trick

Blow up a balloon as hard as you can. Put it into a warm place, such as an airing cupboard. What do you think will happen? Warn your family that there might be a bang!

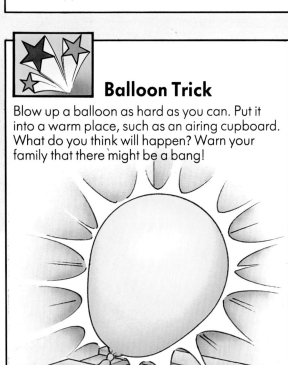

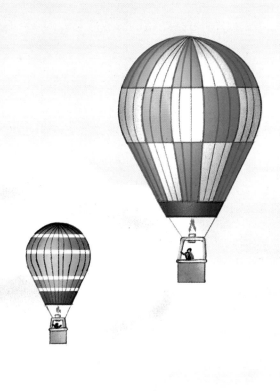

Using Hot Air

If balloons are filled with hot air, they become lighter than the air around them and float up into the air. Modern hot-air balloons have a gas burner to heat the air inside them. The wind blows the balloons along.

Today, balloons are usually filled with helium, which is lighter than air. Balloons are used for a variety of purposes, which range from advertising to carrying scientific instruments high up into the atmosphere. These instruments collect information about the weather and air pollution.

Make a Hot Air Balloon

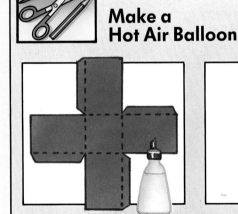

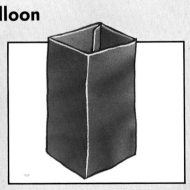

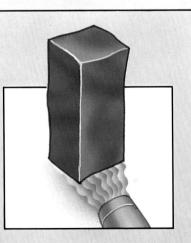

1. Glue 5 sheets of tissue paper together as shown in the diagram. (You need 1 square and 4 rectangles.)

2. Glue together the long sides of each rectangular sheet to make a balloon shape.

3. Inflate your balloon with hot air from a hair drier and it should float up to the ceiling.

Keeping Warm

Warm things cool down fast if they are left in cold air because heat travels from the warm objects into the cold air. Cold draughts make you shiver because your body loses heat to the surrounding air.

Clothes help people to keep warm. Each layer of clothing traps a layer of warm air. In very cold places, people use jackets and sleeping bags with feathers inside them. The feathers trap a lot of air and keep the people warm.

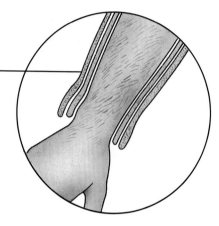

Air is trapped between layers of clothing.

Cooling Down

Remove the lids from the four jars and wrap them up as shown in the diagrams to the right. Fill each jar with hot water and put the lid back on. Cover the lid with same wrapping as the rest of the jar. Leave the jars in a cool room for about half an hour and then take the temperature of the water with a thermometer or test the water with your little finger. Which jar contains the warmest water?

Equipment: Four jars with lids, hot water, newspaper, scarves or a blanket, thermometer, a box.

1. Put one jar in a box and wrap newspaper loosely around it.

2. Wrap a layer of newspaper around another jar. Hold the newspaper in place with elastic bands.

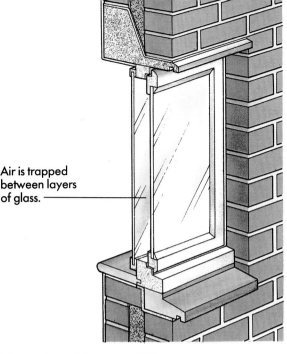

Air is trapped between layers of glass.

Keeping Houses Warm

Houses also lose heat to the surrounding air when the weather is cold. Most of the heat escapes through windows, doors and the roof. People keep their homes warm by sealing gaps around doors and windows and fitting double-glazed windows. These windows trap a layer of air between two panes of glass. This separates the warm air inside from the cold air outside and makes it more difficult for heat to escape.

3. Wrap the third jar loosely in the scarf or blanket.

4. Leave one jar without any wrapping so you can see how much effect the different wrappings have.

How it works

The warmest jar is the one that has been protected from the cool air in the most efficient way. This protection is called **insulation**. The insulation works by keeping a layer of air trapped between the warm water and the cool air outside. This helps to stop the heat escaping. The blanket or scarf and the loosely-packed newspaper both provide good insulation so the water in these jars stays warmer than the water in the other two jars.

People put insulating material in the roofs and walls of houses or wrap these materials around pipes or tanks to stop the heat escaping.

Air Pressure

When you swim underwater you can feel water pushing on your body. The air all around you does the same but your body is used to it so you do not even notice. There is more than a kilogram of air pressing on every square centimetre of your skin. The pressure is caused by a layer of air called the **atmosphere**, which surrounds the Earth. Most of the air is concentrated about 5 kilometres (3 miles) above the surface of the Earth.

▲ Many instruments in an aircraft use changes in air pressure to give important information to the pilot. Air pressure decreases with height and this registers on an instrument called an **altimeter**, which shows how high the aircraft is flying.

Make a Barometer

Air pressure is measured by an instrument called a **barometer**. When air pressure rises, it is usually a sign that the weather is going to improve. Air pressure falls when bad weather is approaching.

Equipment: A tall, **narrow**, clear plastic bottle, a bowl of water, paper, sticky tape, ruler, string, modelling clay.

1. Put a piece of modelling clay on one side of the bowl and use it to hold the ruler upright.
2. Fill the bowl with about 5–8 cm (2–3 inches) of water and fill the bottle three-quarters full of water.
3. Cover the opening of the bottle with the palm of your hand. Then turn the bottle carefully upside down and put the opening under the surface of the water in the dish.
4. Take your hand away from the opening but keep the bottle upright with your other hand. Tie the bottle to the ruler with the string.
5. Mark a piece of paper with a scale and stick it onto the bottle. Make a note of the water level and keep a record of how the level changes from day to day.

How it works
Air presses down on the surface of the water in the bowl. If the air pressure (the pushing power of the air) rises, more water is pushed into the bottle and the level on the scale will go up slightly. If the air pressure falls, the opposite happens.

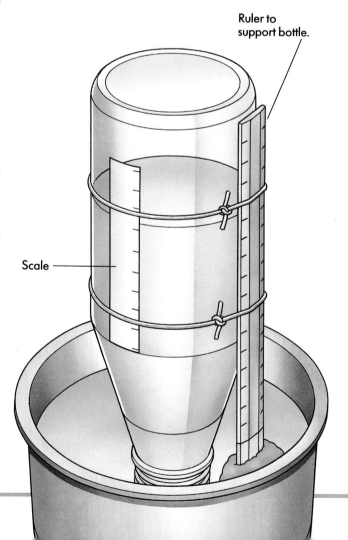

Ruler to support bottle.

Scale

The Power of Air

Air pressure is a powerful force. Here is a trick to prove it. All you need is a ruler, a large sheet of paper and a table.

Lay the ruler on the table so about one third of it lies over the edge. Spread the paper over the ruler. Now hit the ruler and try to make the paper fly into the air. You will find that it is impossible! (Don't hit the ruler too hard or it might break.)

How it works
The air presses down on the sheet of paper. Because the paper has a large area, there is a lot of air pushing down on it and this is enough to stop the paper and the ruler from moving.

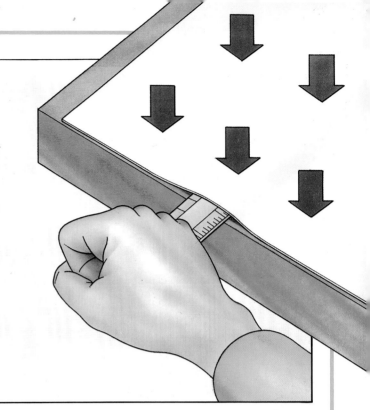

The Magic Glass

The pushing power of air can even keep water in a glass that is upside down! For this trick you will need a glass with a smooth rim, water and a piece of smooth card about the size of a postcard.

Fill the glass right up to the top with water and wet the rim slightly. Lay the card on top of the glass. Hold the card firmly in place and turn the glass over. Now take away your hand. The water should stay in the glass. Don't give up if it doesn't work first time – try again until you succeed.

Hint: Make sure you have a good seal between the glass and the card before you turn it upside down. It is a good idea to try this trick over a sink first!

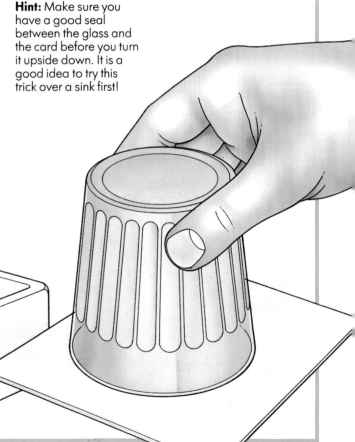

Make a Fountain

Equipment: Two glass jars (one with a lid), a bottle of water, modelling clay, four plastic straws (or a plastic tube), sticky tape, a bowl.

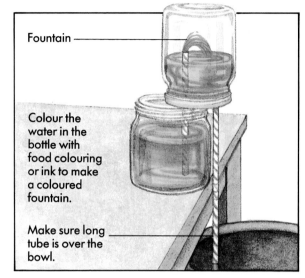

Fountain

Colour the water in the bottle with food colouring or ink to make a coloured fountain.

Make sure long tube is over the bowl.

Seal gaps around straws.

1. Make two holes in the lid.
2. Push a straw through one hole so about 5 cm (2 inches) shows inside the lid. Make a long tube by fixing three straws together with sticky tape (or use plastic tubing) and push one end of the long tube through the other hole in the lid.
3. Seal the gaps between the straws (or tubing) and the lid with modelling clay.
4. Put about 5 cm (2 inches) of water into one of the jars and screw on the lid.

5. Fill the second jar three-quarters full of water and place it on the edge of a table. Position the bowl underneath. Turn the jar with the straws in the lid upside down and dip the short straw into the jar of water on the table. As you do this a fountain of water should rise up the straw.

How it works
As water from the closed jar pours down into the bowl through the longer straw (or tube), the air pressure inside the jar becomes less as the air spreads out to take up the space left by the water. The air outside is at a greater pressure than the air inside and pushes down on the water in the open jar. This forces the water up the short straw and makes the fountain.

How Straws Work

When you suck through a straw, you lower the pushing power of the air in your mouth and in the straw. The air pushing down on the surface of your drink forces liquid up the straw.

You can test this for yourself. Drink some liquid and notice how easily it comes up the straw. Then make a small hole in the straw about 5 cm (2 inches) from the top end and try to drink again. Some liquid will rise up the straw as you suck but air rushing in through the hole will try to push the liquid down again. You will be able to drink but it will take much longer and you will suck in bubbles of air too!

The Egg and Bottle Trick

Equipment: A cooked egg without the shell, a bottle with a neck slightly smaller than the egg, a piece of paper, a match or taper.

1. Check that the egg will just fit into the neck of the bottle but will not fall through. (The wide-necked bottles – carafes – that are used to serve wine are about right.)

2. Screw up the piece of paper and put it into the bottle.

3. Light the paper by using a long taper or dropping a burning match into the bottle.

4. Quickly fit the egg into the neck of the bottle. Amazingly, the egg will be sucked into the bottle with a gurgle and a pop!

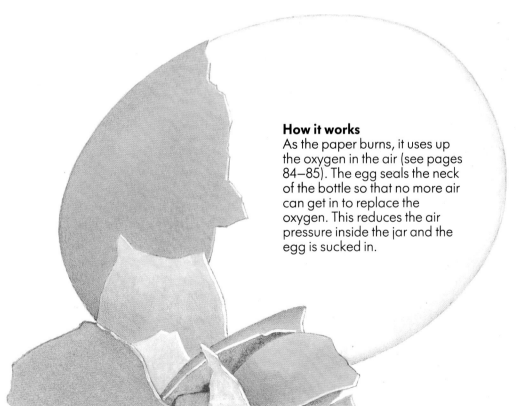

How it works
As the paper burns, it uses up the oxygen in the air (see pages 84–85). The egg seals the neck of the bottle so that no more air can get in to replace the oxygen. This reduces the air pressure inside the jar and the egg is sucked in.

Air on the Move

When air moves, it has less pushing power and does not press on objects as much as still air. Objects look as if they are sucked into a stream of moving air but in fact they are pushed into the air stream by the stronger pressure of the other air around them. Objects can be pushed into the fast-moving air of a hurricane with great force.

 ## Amazing Apples

Hang up two apples about 5 cm (2 inches) apart and steady them so they hang still. Blow hard between the apples and try to separate them.

 ## Blow the Paper Away

Place two large books about 10 cm (4 inches) apart on a table. Lay a sheet of paper over the books. Try to get the paper to float away by blowing underneath it. Can you do it? You will find that the paper droops down in the middle as you blow.

Can you work out why this happens?

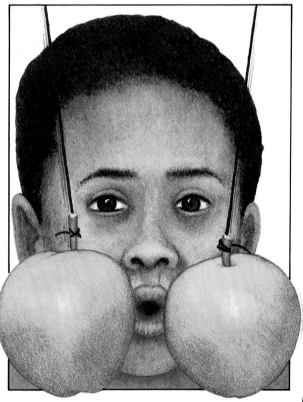

Surprisingly, the apples move towards each other! As you blow, you move the air between the apples. This moving air has less pushing power than the air on the side of the apples. So the pushing power of the air outside the apples makes them move together.

More things to try

If you are still not convinced, try the same trick using two sheets of paper. Hold them in front of your face and try to blow them apart. Once again, the moving air you blow between them should draw the sheets of paper together instead of separating them.

Make a Plant Sprayer

Use the spray to water your plants.

Equipment: 2 plastic straws, a glass of water.

1. Stand one of the straws upright in the water. It should be a little taller than the glass (trim the straw if it is too long).
2. Hold the second straw at right angles to the first one, as shown in the diagram.
3. Blow through the second straw and watch the level of water in the first straw.
If you blow gently, you will see the water rise a little. If you blow very hard, the water will rise to the top of the straw and form a spray.

How it works
The moving air blowing across the top of the straw has less pushing power than still air. The air pressing down on the water in the glass is able to push harder than the moving air and forces water up the straw.

▶ Perfume sprayers work in the same way as the plant sprayer above. The air is moved by squeezing a bulb of air.

Jumping Counter Trick

This trick shows how strong winds can lift things from the ground. All you need is a saucer and a counter.

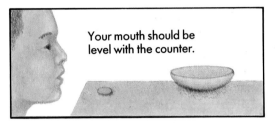

Your mouth should be level with the counter.

Place the counter about 1 cm (½ inch) from the edge of a table. Set the saucer a little way beyond it.

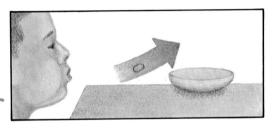

Blow strongly across the top of the counter. With some practice, you should be able to lift the counter into the saucer.

More things to try
You can make the trick more fun by drawing a target with scores and challenging your friends to a game.

Air Streams

In 1738, a Swiss scientist called Bernoulli discovered that moving air has less pushing power than still air. He did not realize that one day his idea would be used to lift aircraft into the sky.

Make a Wing

This experiment will help you to understand how an aircraft wing is designed to lift such a heavy machine into the air.

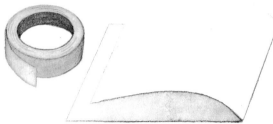

Fold a small piece of paper in half and tape the top half to the bottom half about 2.5 cm (1 inch) from the edge. (This will make the top surface curved.) Slide the ruler into the fold of the wing. Then blow to direct a stream of air towards the wing. You will see the wing rise into the air as you blow.

Lift a Paper Strip

Hold a sheet of thin paper in front of your face just below your lips. Blow steadily over the top of the paper. What happens?

Your breath moves the air above the paper, which reduces the pushing power of that air. The air pressure underneath the paper remains normal and this stronger air pressure lifts the paper.

Air flow speeds up so air pressure is low.

Air flow is normal so higher air pressure pushes wing upwards.

The air flowing over the curved surface on the top of the wing moves faster than the air underneath the wing. This makes the air pressure above the wing lower than the pressure underneath. The greater pressure underneath the wing pushes it up into the air. The wings on an aircraft are a similar shape to help them lift the plane off the ground (see pages 76–77).

Hovering Card Trick

Equipment: A cotton reel, an 8 cm (3 inch) square of light card, a drawing pin.

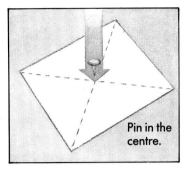

Pin in the centre.

1. Join the corners of the card with diagonal lines across the square. The point where the lines cross is the centre of the card.
2. Push the drawing pin through the centre of the card.
3. Hold the card under the cotton reel so the drawing pin is in the hole.
4. Lift the card and the cotton reel and blow hard down the hole. Take your hand away. Can you blow the card off the reel?

How it works
The stream of air you blow down the reel passes between the reel and the card. This moving air has less pushing power than the air below the card and so the card is pushed up onto the reel.

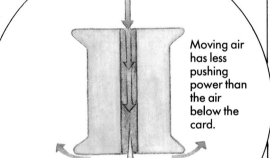

Moving air has less pushing power than the air below the card.

Air pressure pushes card upwards.

Hiding from the Wind

Have you ever tried to shelter from the wind behind a tree? This experiment will show you why it does not always give you much protection.

1. Fix a candle firmly to a saucer, place it on a table and light it.
2. Place a bottle in front of the candle.
3. Blow from behind the bottle towards the candle and watch what happens to the flame.

The flame will go out because the stream of air joins up again on the other side of the bottle with the same strength as before.

More things to try
● Move the candle a short distance from the bottle. What happens now?
● Remove the bottle and blow down a funnel. Can you explain what happens to the flame?

You could ask a friend to tell you what happens to the candle flame.

Fly Through the Air

Paper darts fly well. Their streamlined shape makes them shoot through the air and you can throw them accurately for a long way if they are carefully folded. Racing cars and fighter aircraft have a smooth, slim, streamlined shape to help them move rapidly. Air can flow easily over their bodywork and does not hold them back.

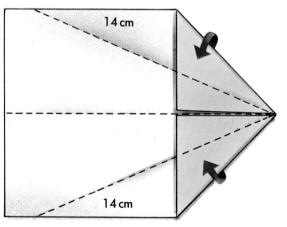

Making Paper Darts

All you need to investigate streamlining is two pieces of paper about 30 cm (1 foot) × 20 cm (8 inches).

Take one piece of paper and try throwing it. You will find it only travels a short distance before it floats to the ground. Next squash the same piece of paper into a ball. This time the paper should travel quite a long distance when you throw it. But its shape soon makes it sink to the ground.

Now make a paper dart by folding the other piece of paper as shown in the diagrams below.
How long will your dart stay in the air?
How far can you throw it?

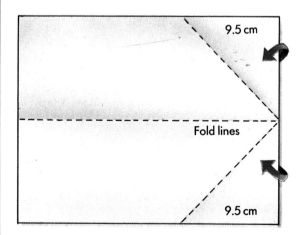

9.5 cm

Fold lines

9.5 cm

14 cm

14 cm

1. Measure the centre of the shortest side of the paper and draw a line down the middle. Measure 9.5 cm (4 inches) down each side and draw a line to the top of the paper.

2. Fold along the lines you have just drawn. Then measure 14cm (5½ inches) further down and draw two more lines to the centre of the paper at the top.

▶ The streamlined shape of Concorde helps it to fly at 2333 kilometres per hour (1450 miles per hour) – faster than a rifle bullet. Concorde can fly across the Atlantic Ocean in just three hours.

More things to try

- Curve up the top surfaces of the wings. This should help the dart to fly for longer.
- Make flaps at the back of the wings. You may have seen flaps on aircraft wings. They are used to help in landing and turning the plane. The flaps on your dart should make it roll as it flies.
- Weight the nose of the dart with a paperclip. What difference does the extra weight make?

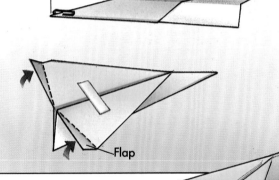

Paper clip

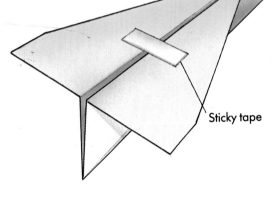

Flap

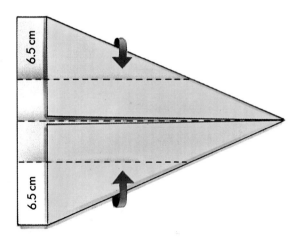

6.5 cm

6.5 cm

Sticky tape

3. Fold along this second line as shown. Then measure 6.5 cm (2½ inches) from each side of the bottom edge of the paper and draw a line straight up to the top.

4. Fold away from you along the centre line and towards you on the two lines on either side of the centre line. Fix the wings in position with sticky tape.

Squashing Air

If you pump up a tyre, it begins to fill with air. As you keep pumping, you force in more and more air. Inside the tyre, the air is squashed into a small space. This is called **compressed air**. It has great strength and can support bicycles and cars.

▲ Compressed air is strong enough to break up concrete. It is used to power drills.

Compressed air

◄ Hold your finger over the end of a bicycle pump as you push the handle down. As you squash the air into a smaller space, it becomes harder to push the handle down.

Lifting Books With Air

Show a pile of heavy books to your friends and ask if they can lift them using only their breath. Impossible they will say! Then show them how it can be done.

Lay a large plastic bag on a table and pile the books on top. Leave the open end of the bag sticking out. Blow into the bag keeping the opening as small as possible. Take your time and you will see the books rise off the table. They are supported by the compressed air in the bag.

Make a Helicopter

Compressed air helps a helicopter to lift off the ground. As the rotors on the top of the helicopter spin round, they push air down. This squashes the air under the rotors and the compressed air pushes the helicopter upwards.

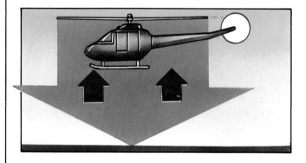

Compressed air pushes helicopter up into the air.

1. To make the rotors, trace over the cross shape on the next page.
2. Fold along the dotted lines as shown. Fold one side of each rotor up and the other side down.
3. Fix the thin stick through the hole in the rotor and stick it firmly with tape or glue.

Make a Rocket

Equipment: A soft plastic bottle (a washing-up liquid bottle will do), 2 plastic straws (one narrower than the other), modelling clay, glue.

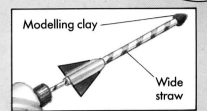

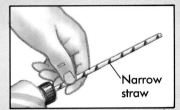

Narrow straw

Modelling clay

Wide straw

1. Make a hole in the cap of the bottle and push the smaller straw through. Seal the joint with modelling clay or glue. This makes the launch pad.

2. Then make the rocket. Cut about 10 cm (4 inches) off the larger straw. Decorate one end with paper triangles. Make a 'nose' for the other end with modelling clay.

3. Slide the rocket over the launch pad. Squeeze the plastic bottle firmly and watch the compressed air in the bottle push the rocket into the air.

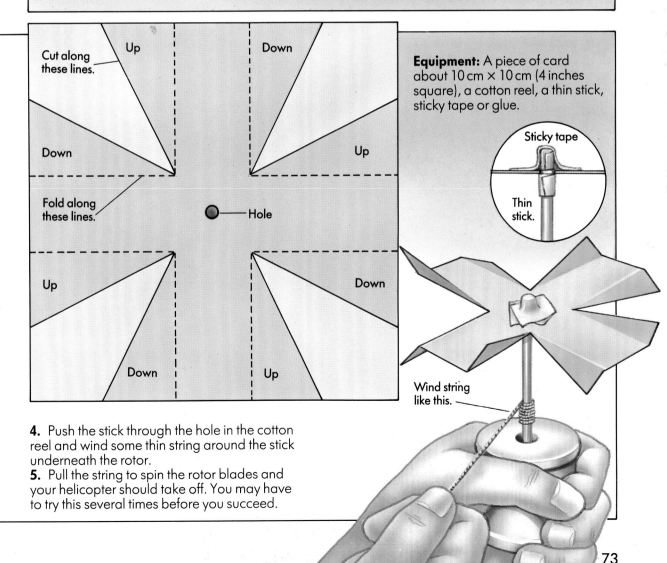

Cut along these lines.

Up

Down

Down

Up

Fold along these lines.

Hole

Up

Down

Down

Up

Equipment: A piece of card about 10 cm × 10 cm (4 inches square), a cotton reel, a thin stick, sticky tape or glue.

Sticky tape

Thin stick.

Wind string like this.

4. Push the stick through the hole in the cotton reel and wind some thin string around the stick underneath the rotor.

5. Pull the string to spin the rotor blades and your helicopter should take off. You may have to try this several times before you succeed.

As a parachute falls, air is trapped inside the 'umbrella' part. This air is squashed (compressed) so it has greater pushing power than the air around. It presses up from under the parachute and pushes it upwards. The push is not strong enough to stop the parachute falling but it does slow it down. Most parachutes are umbrella shaped but some are special shapes or have extra panels to allow parachutists to steer them.

Parachute Tests

Equipment: Paper, string, sticky tape, a small, unbreakable object.

Choose a suitable high place (such as a chair or the side of a staircase) from which to drop the toy or other object to be parachuted. First drop the object and notice how long it takes to fall. Then try dropping it attached to three different kinds of parachutes:

1. A squashed up ball made from a 20 cm (8 inch) square piece of paper.
2. A flat piece of paper the same size as the one you squashed.
3. A piece of paper 35cm (14 inches) square. Which parachute takes the longest time to fall? (Take care to drop the parachutes from the same height each time.)

You should find the largest parachute takes the longest time to fall because it has the most air pushing up underneath it to slow it down.

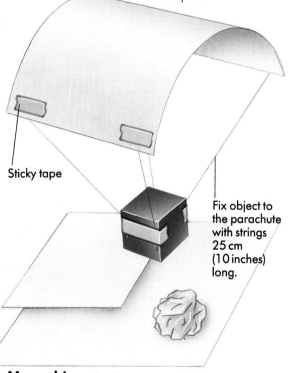

Sticky tape

Fix object to the parachute with strings 25 cm (10 inches) long.

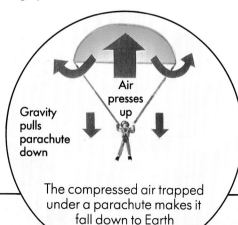

Air presses up

Gravity pulls parachute down

The compressed air trapped under a parachute makes it fall down to Earth slowly.

More things to try
● Longer strings
● A hole in the top of the parachute.
● Different shapes (such as circles).
● Different materials (such as plastic or cotton).

Making a Kite

Kites work in a similar way to parachutes. As a kite is held into the wind, air is squashed under it. This compressed air pushes the kite upwards so it can fly. Kites are made of very light materials so they stay up in the air easily.

Equipment: Thin material about 1 metre × 75 cm (3 feet × 2½ feet), thin sticks, a ball of string, sticky tape, glue, scissors, needle, thread.

1. First choose two sticks to make the framework. The exact measurements are not important but one stick must be twice as long as the other. Make a cross shape with the sticks and bind them together with string. Then join the corners with short sticks or string to make a diamond shape.

2. Lay the frame on top of the piece of material. Carefully cut the material around the frame leaving about 3 or 4 centimetres (1½ inches) all round. Fold over the material to cover the frame and sew or glue down the folds.

3. Make a tail for your kite using a piece of string about twice as long as the kite. Glue or tie the tail to the tip of the kite. Then attach two strings to the long stick of the frame – one above and one below the crossover point. Join the two ends together and tie them on to the end of the ball of string.

String to join corners.

Tie corner pieces in position.

Glue

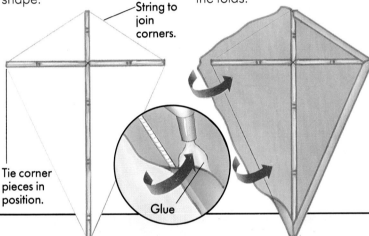

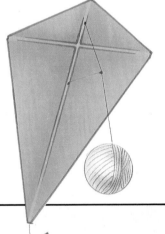

Making a kite fly

On a windy day, you can just hold your kite up into the wind. As you let go, the kite will float upwards, pushed by the air. (Don't forget to unwind the string to stop the kite being pulled down again.) If it is not very windy, you can get your kite to take off by running forwards into a breeze pulling the kite behind you. As you run, air is squashed into the kite and this lifts it up.

Looking at Flight

How do heavy aircraft get off the ground and stay up in the air? The answer is the pushing power of air. An aircraft is able to lift itself off the ground partle due to its speed (which is produced by its powerful engines) and partly due to the shape of its wings.

The smooth, **streamlined** shape of the plane allows air to flow easily over its surface. This helps to reduce the drag caused by the air pushing against the plane and allows it to move rapidly through the air.

How Planes Fly

All planes need air pressure under their wings to stay up in the air. As they move forwards, the higher air pressure underneath their wings pushes them upwards and gives them **lift**.

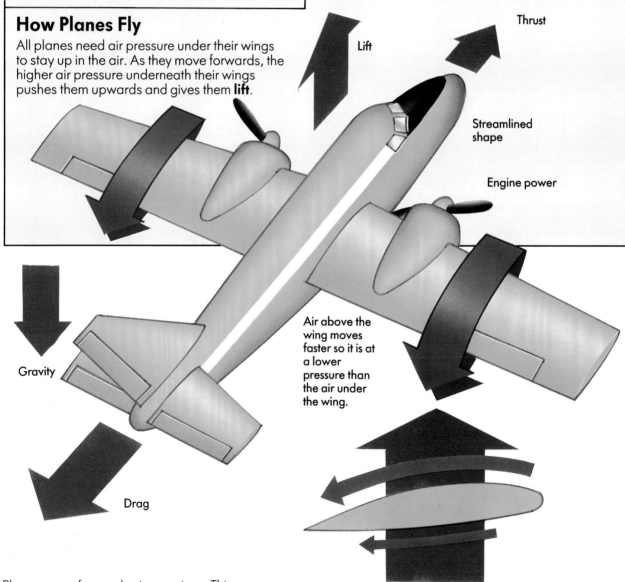

Lift

Thrust

Streamlined shape

Engine power

Gravity

Air above the wing moves faster so it is at a lower pressure than the air under the wing.

Drag

Planes move forward using engines. This movement is called **thrust**. Moving forwards keeps a stream of moving air passing over the wings, which allows the plane to stay up in the air. If the engines fail, the plane will begin to descend very quickly.

Air under the wing moves more slowly and is slightly squashed so it is a at higher pressure than the air above the wing.

Diving

Two small panels (called **elevators**) on the tailplane are lowered. This pushes the tail up and the nose down. To make the plane climb, the elevators are raised.

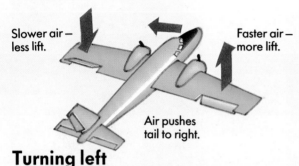

Slower air — less lift.

Faster air flow creates more lift.

Faster air — more lift.

Air pushes tail to right.

Turning left

The rudder is moved to the left and a panel (called an **aileron**) on the left wing is lifted up. The aileron on the right wing is moved down.

How Birds Fly

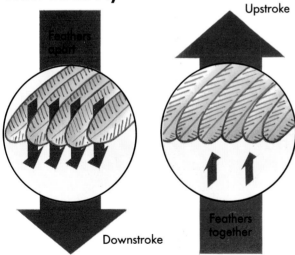

Upstroke

Feathers apart

Downstroke

Feathers together

Most birds can fly. They use their wings, feathers and feet to do all the things a plane does with its wings and engines. During take-off, a bird pushes down with its wings and its feet to produce **'thrust'** and **'lift'**. The feathers on a bird's wing are arranged so that the top surface curves upwards. This helps to give extra 'lift' by making the air on the upper surface of the wings move faster.

Engines

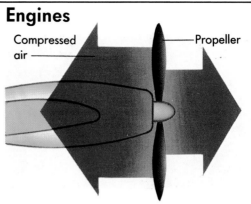

Compressed air

Propeller

Some planes have propeller engines. As the propeller blades turn, they squash (**compress**) the air behind them and the pressure of this air pushes the plane forwards.

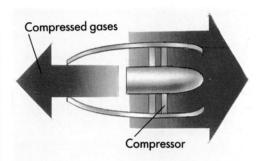

Compressed gases

Compressor

Jet engines suck in air at the front and, as their fuel burns, they shoot out very hot, compressed exhaust gases at the back. These gases are at high pressure and push the plane forwards.

Wind and Weather

Changes in temperature and pressure make large sections of the air move about. This moving air is called the wind. The direction of the wind and the speed at which it moves affects our weather. Information about the wind is gathered from weather stations, ships and satellites out in space. The data are used to predict the weather.

▶ Look out for unusual wind vanes. This one is on the top of a church steeple.

Make a Wind Vane

Equipment: Modelling clay, carton, pencil with eraser, pin, straw, card, sticky tape.

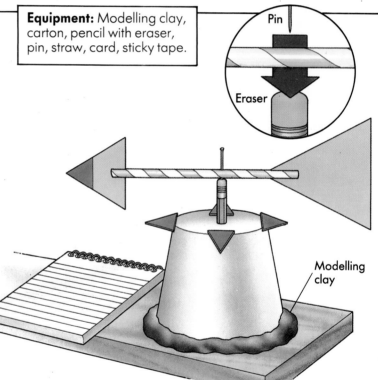

Pin

Eraser

Modelling clay

1. Make a hole in the middle of the bottom of the yoghurt carton and push the pencil into the hole.
2. Fix the carton to the thick card with modelling clay.
3. Cut two small triangles of thin card and fix one in each end of the straw.
4. Push the pin through the middle of the straw and into the eraser.
5. Put the wind vane on a flat surface outside. Use a compass to mark north, south, east and west on the carton. (If you do not have a compass, look at the Sun. It rises in the east and sets in the west.)

Push pencil through hole in carton.

Make slits in straw and glue triangles in position.

Use the information from your wind vane to make a chart showing which direction the wind is blowing **from** each day. Weather forecasters always talk about the direction that the wind is blowing **from**. A west wind blows from the west to the east, for example. Does the direction of the wind affect the weather in your area?

How Fast Does the Wind Move?

In 1806, an English admiral called Sir Francis Beaufort worked out a scale from 0–12 to indicate the strength of the wind. His scale was based on the effect of the wind on objects such as trees and houses. The speed of the wind was added later. The scale is used today if there are no instruments available to measure wind speed.

The strongest winds on the scale are called hurricanes, typhoons or cyclones. They travel at more than 150 kilometres per hour (93 miles per hour).

Force: 0 **Strength**: Calm
Speed: Under 4 kph
Effect: Smoke goes straight up.

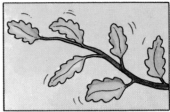

Force: 1–3 **Strength**: Light breeze
Speed: 4–24 kph
Effect: Small branches move.

Force: 4–5 **Strength**: Moderate wind
Speed: 25–46 kph
Effect: Small trees sway a little.

Force: 6–7 **Strength**: Strong wind
Speed: 47–74 kph
Effect: Big trees sway a little.

Force: 8–9 **Strength**: Gale
Speed: 75–110 kph
Effect: Slates fall off.

Force: 10–11 **Strength**: Storm
Speed: 111–150 kph
Effect: Widespread damage.

Force: 12 **Strength**: Hurricane
Speed: Above 150 kph
Effect: Disaster.

► A dramatic view of a typhoon taken from a satellite out in space. Typhoons are violent hurricanes in the China seas. The name 'typhoon' may either come from the Chinese words *tai fung* (which mean 'wind which strikes') or from the Greek monster *Typhoeus*, who was the father of storm winds.

Catching the Wind

People have invented different ways of catching the wind and using its power to push boats along or drive machines, such as windmills. You can find out more about the power of moving air by making your own windmills and boats.

▲ Windmills in the Netherlands.

Make a Windmill

Equipment: Thin card or stiff paper, the top of a washing-up liquid bottle, a stick, a nail 38 mm (1½ inches) long.

1. Trace this shape onto the thin card. Mark on the lines and dots.
2. Cut along the dotted lines and make holes through the dots.
3. Bend the four corners over and stick them together with glue.

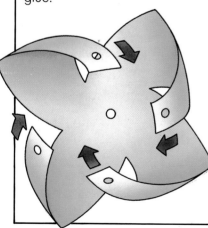

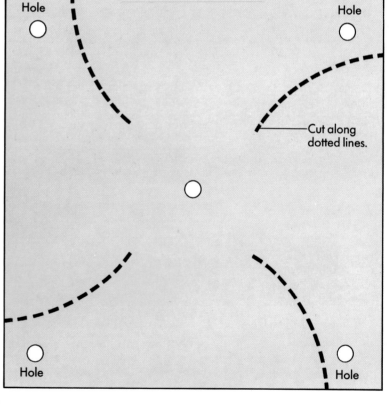

Hole

Hole

Cut along dotted lines.

Hole

Hole

Make a
Sailing Boat

Equipment: A matchbox (or thin card), cocktail sticks or toothpicks, modelling clay, paper, scissors, bowl of water.

▼ Modern sailing boats have special sails to catch the wind blowing in all directions so they can move along very rapidly.

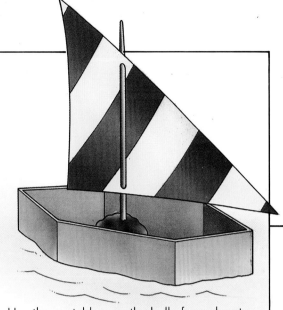

Use the matchbox as the hull of your boat (or make the hull out of thin card). Cut a sail shape from the paper and fix it to the boat using a cocktail stick or toothpick and modelling clay. Float the boat on some water and blow into the sail to make the boat move.

More things to try

Blow from different directions and see how the boat moves. Make different shaped sails for your boat. Do larger sails work better than small ones? What happens if you put two sails on your boat?

Bottle top

5. Push the nail through the middle of the washing-up liquid cap and ask an adult to hammer it into the stick.

Bend nail over at the back.

4. Fix the top of the washing-up liquid bottle into the middle of the windmill and push the small end through the back of the windmill.

What happens when you blow on the windmill? Does it work better when you blow from the front or from the side? Put it outside so you can see how fast the wind is blowing.

Air and Burning

Fires will not burn without air. If a fire does not burn well, people sometimes blow on it or fan the flames so that more air reaches the fire. Fires are very dangerous so be extra careful if you do any experiments that involve fire or flames and always ask an adult to help you.

Does All the Air Burn?

Air is used up when things burn. But only part of the air is used for burning. Try an investigation to prove this.

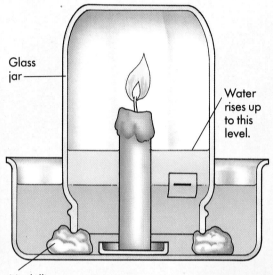

Glass jar

Water rises up to this level.

Modelling clay

Equipment: Candle, modelling clay, bowl of water, large glass jar, matches.

Place the candle on its saucer or lid in a bowl of water. Make sure the candle is tall enough to be well clear of the water surface. Light the candle and cover it with the glass jar. Rest the jar on modelling clay so water can get under the rim. Mark the level of water in the jar. The candle will burn for a time but will eventually go out and you will see that the water rises up into the jar. You will find it rises about one fifth of the way up the jar.

How it works
When the candle burned, it only used part of the air in the jar. In fact it used only the gas called oxygen, which makes up about one fifth of the air. When the oxygen was used up, the flame went out and water was pushed up into the jar by the pressure of air outside. Oxygen is the part of the air that people need to live and breathe (see pages 84–85). The rest of the air is mainly a gas called nitrogen.

Three Candle Race

Warning: Make sure you put out the candle that wins the race.

Fix three candles firmly to three saucers or lids using modelling clay. Place them in a safe place on a table and light the candles. Leave one candle open to the air, cover one candle with a small jar and one with a large jar. Which candle burns for the longest time?

How it works
The candle with lots of air around it can keep burning after both the candles in the jars have gone out. The candle in the large jar has more air around it so it will burn for longer than the candle in the small jar.

82

Make a Fire Extinguisher

Vinegar

Bicarbonate of soda.

Equipment: A glass, a candle, a saucer, matches, a teaspoon, vinegar, bicarbonate of soda, a cardboard tube.

Carbon dioxide rolls down tube onto candle.

1. Fix the candle to the saucer or lid and place it on a table. Light the candle.

2. Put one teaspoonful of bicarbonate of soda into the glass. Pour in about 3 cm (1 inch) of vinegar. You will see bubbles appear in the glass. These are a gas called carbon dioxide, which is formed as the vinegar and bicarbonate of soda mix together.

▼ Foam from fire extinguishers keeps oxygen away from the flames by covering them in a blanket of bubbles of carbon dioxide gas. Carbon dioxide does not burn.

3. To put out the candle, carefully tip the carbon dioxide gas down the cardboard tube. You will not be able to see the gas but just imagine you are pouring water down the tube. Keep the end of the tube out of the candle flame.

4. As the carbon dioxide covers the flame it will soon go out.

How it works
Carbon dioxide is heavier than air, which is why you are able to pour it down the tube. It pushes the oxygen away from the candle flame and stops it burning.

Air for Life

All living things need the oxygen in the air to survive. If people travel to places where there is not enough air (such as the tops of mountains) or no air at all (such as out in space) they have to take a supply of air with them. People also have to take air underwater with them.

The Air You Breathe

People get the oxygen they need by breathing. As you breathe in, you take air into the lungs in your chest. Inside the lungs, oxygen passes into the blood and is carried all round the body. It is used in the chemical reactions that release energy from food. The waste gas (carbon dioxide) produced in this reaction leaves your body as you breathe out. Count how many times you breathe every minute. How does this change after exercise, such as running or cycling?

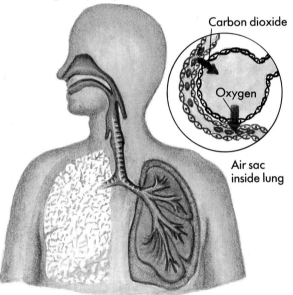

Carbon dioxide

Oxygen

Air sac inside lung

◀ There is no air in space so astronauts have to take it with them. If they leave the spacecraft, they breathe air from special cylinders on their backs.

How Much Air Do Your Lungs Hold?

1. Put the bowl in the sink or the bath and fill it about one third full of water. Fill the bottle to the top with water.
2. Place the palm of your hand over the top of the bottle (or put the stopper on). Quickly turn the bottle upside down and put the top under the surface of the water in the bowl. Ask someone to hold the bottle steady and take your hand away (or remove the stopper).
3. Fix a ruler to the side of the bottle with elastic bands or mark a scale on some paper and stick it onto the bottle.
4. Put the tube in the neck of the bottle. Take a deep breath, hold your nose and blow hard down the tube. How much water can you blow out in one go? This will give you some idea how much air is in your lungs.

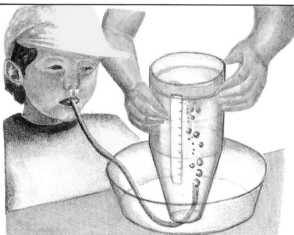

Equipment: A large plastic bottle that holds 4 or 5 litres (7 or 9 pints) of water (such as a camping container), plastic tubing 60 cm (2 feet) long, ruler, elastic bands, bowl.

Where Does Oxygen Come From?

Green plants are very important for life on Earth because they produce oxygen. (This is why it is important for us to take care of our environment and not to cut down large areas of forest.) Green plants produce oxygen during the process they use to make their own food from carbon dioxide (another gas in the air) and water. Energy from the Sun is used to power this process, which is called **photosynthesis** – this means 'making things with light'.

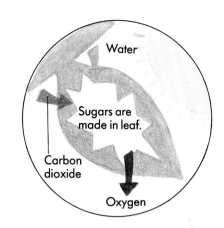

Photosynthesis takes place mainly in the leaves of green plants. Try this experiment to prove that oxygen is released. All you need is a bowl of water, a glass jar and some water plants such as pondweed. Place the plants in the bowl of water. Fill the glass jar with water by lowering it into the bowl on its side. Turn it upside down to cover the plants. Leave the experiment in a sunny place and look at it from time to time.

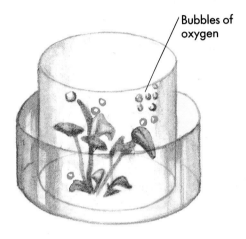

How it works

You will notice streams of oxygen bubbles rising to the surface of the water. Eventually a little pocket of oxygen will collect at the top of the jar. Water plants release oxygen into the water just as land plants release oxygen into the air.

How Polluted is the Air?

Car exhausts, factories and power stations produce smoke, gases and dust, which make the air dirty and polluted. Tiny plants called **lichens** can show you how polluted the air is. Some types of lichen grow where the air is polluted; others can only survive in clean air. The air is cleanest where there are a lot of different types of lichen. Look for lichens on trees and walls.

Polluted air → Clean air

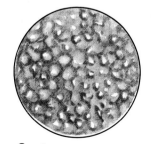

No lichens
An alga called *Pleurococcus* forms a powdery green film on trees and walls. This is a sign the air is polluted.

Crusty, grey or green lichens
These lichens grow in town centres and can survive where the air is dirty.

Flat, rounded lichens
These may be green, yellow, black or orange and can survive some pollution.

Bushy lichens
Usually green or grey. These are very sensitive to air pollution and will grow only where the air is clean.

Air and Sound

Air does not only carry aircraft and birds, it also carries sounds. You may be surprised to learn that there is no sound out in space, where there is no air.

Sounds travel through air rather like ripples travel across a pond. If you throw a stone into a calm pond, the water near the stone moves up and down and ripples travel outwards. If the ripples bump against a small object, such as a stick floating on the water, they will make the object move up and down as well. In a similar way, sounds make the air close to them move up and down in waves. This is called **vibration**. If the vibration of the air reaches your ears, it makes the ear drum inside each ear vibrate so you can hear the sounds.

Make a Harp

All you need is a cardboard or plastic box and eight, thick elastic bands. Stretch the elastic bands around the box and pull the bands with your fingers to play your 'harp'. Then put your fingers on the end of a band to stretch it tighter. The tighter the elastic band, the higher the note it makes.

Sound Waves

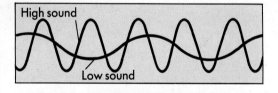

High sounds make waves that are close together. Low sounds make waves that are further apart. Just as with ripples on a pond, sound waves become weaker further away from a sound. This is why you can hear more easily when you are close to the source of a sound.

Making Music

Musical instruments make sounds in a number of different ways. Each one starts the air vibrating in its own way.

Vibrations from a drum begin when the skin stretched across the surface of the drum is hit with a special stick. The skin moves up and down and starts the flow of sound waves. Instruments with strings, such as guitars or violins, are plucked with a bow or fingers to start a stream of vibrations. Woodwind instruments have a mouthpiece. The player either blows down into the instrument to make a reed vibrate (as with an oboe or clarinet) or blows across a hole to make a column of air inside the instrument vibrate (as with a flute).

Fix a cork to a knitting needle and push it inside a cardboard tube. Blow across the top of the tube and move the needle up and down. What happens? This is how the sound is produced in a flute.

Singing Bottles

Arrange several bottles in a row. Leave the first one empty and put a small amount of water in the next one along. Put a little more water in the third bottle, even more in the fourth one and so on until you get to the end of the row. Fill the last bottle almost to the top. Tap the bottles with the spoon or blow across the top. As you tap on the glass or blow across the top of the bottle, you make the air inside vibrate. There is a different amount of air in each bottle so each one makes a different sound.

How Far Away is the Storm?

During a storm, have you ever noticed that you always see lightning before you hear thunder? When lightning flashes, it suddenly releases a great amount of heat. This warms the air, which expands with a small explosion that we call thunder. We see the lightning almost immediately because light travels fast. But the sound waves from the thunder take longer to reach our ears.

When you see lightning, count the number of seconds before you hear the thunder. Divide the number of seconds by three and this will tell you approximately how far away the storm is in kilometres.

Air Quiz

True or False?

Hovercraft

Helicopter

1. These machines both use compressed air to help them travel.

2. This plant is producing oxygen.

3. Several layers of clothing will keep you warmer than one thick item of clothing.

True or False?

4. When the air pressure rises, it is usually a sign of bad weather.

Spot the mistakes

Helium

Air

7. What is wrong with these pictures?

5. Which one of these parachutes will fall more quickly?

6. Which one of these bottles will produce a higher sound if you tap it with a spoon?

Answers

1. *True.* Compressed air pushes helicopters up into the sky (pages 72 and 75), and hovercraft travel on a cushion of compressed air.

2. *False.* Plants release oxygen during photosynthesis, which only occurs during the day (page 85).

3. *True. Each layer of clothing traps a layer of warm air (page 60).*

4. *False.* Rising pressure is usually a sign of better weather (page 62).

5. *The smaller parachute will fall more quickly because it has less air pressing up underneath it to slow it down (page 74).*

6. *The bottle with less air inside (page 87).*

7. *Top: Helium is lighter than air so the scale should not balance (page 54).*
Bottom: The paper should not blow away. Moving air has less pressure than still air so the paper is pressed down by the higher pressure of the air above it (page 66).

MOVING

This section of the book will help you to investigate the way things move. Think about different kinds of movement when you use a see-saw or a slide or watch machines such as cranes, washing machines or steam engines working.

This section covers seven main topics:

- Gravity and weight
- Balancing
- Inertia
- Friction
- Slopes, wheels, pulleys and levers
- Different types of movement
- Machines and movement

Use the symbols below to help you identify the three kinds of practical activities in this book.

EXPERIMENTS

TRICKS

THINGS TO MAKE

Introduction

Pushing, pulling, lifting, stretching, twisting and spinning are just some of the different types of movement you can explore in this book. Objects cannot move by themselves; they need a force to push or pull them before they can start or stop moving. It takes more force to make things start or stop than it does to keep them moving.

A natural force called gravity pulls things down to the ground but people have invented a number of machines to make things move in different directions and at different speeds. Rollers, wheels, levers, pulleys and gears all make it easier to move a heavy load. Even the most complex machines have simple levers and wheels somewhere inside them.

The questions on these two pages are based on some of the scientific ideas explained in this book. As you carry out the experiments and tricks you will be able to answer these questions and understand more about how things move in the world around you.

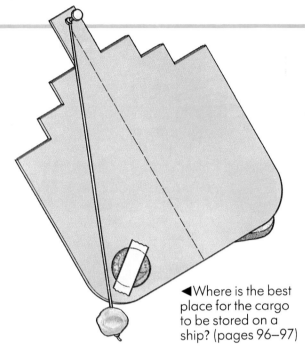

◀Where is the best place for the cargo to be stored on a ship? (pages 96–97)

▼Why do wheels make it easier to move quickly? (p.110–111)

▶Why do pulleys make it easier to lift a heavy weight? (pages 112–113)

▼Why do bowling alleys have a smooth, shiny floor? (pages 104–107)

▲How does a water wheel produce enough power to grind wheat into flour? (pages 124–125)

▲Why do apples fall **down** from the tree? (pages 92–93)

▼ What makes a see-saw balance? (pages 98–99)

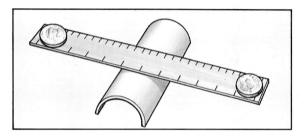

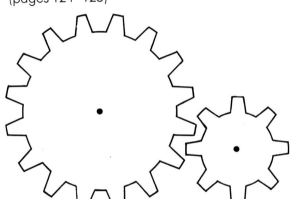

◄Why do gear wheels make machines move quickly and easily? (page 111)

◄Why does oiling a bicycle make it go faster? (pages 106–107)

▼Why do gloves make it easier for a goalkeeper to hold on to the ball? (page 105)

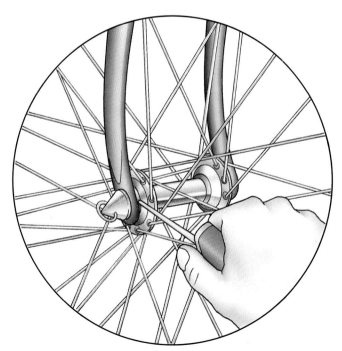

Down to Earth

When an apple falls from a tree, why does it fall **down** to the ground? A famous scientist called Isaac Newton puzzled over this problem while sitting in an orchard many years ago. He suggested that the apple and the Earth both had an invisible force that pulled other objects towards them. But the Earth was so large and had such a powerful force it was able to pull the apple down to the ground. This force around objects is called **gravity**.

Investigating Falling

In the 1590s, a scientist called Galileo put forward the theory that all objects are pulled down to Earth at the same speed no matter what they weigh.

Try to prove Galileo's theory for yourself. All you need is a heavy ball bearing and a marble, a tin tray and a chair. Place the tray on the floor and stand on the chair above the tray. Hold the ball bearing in one hand and the marble in the other. Hold your arms as high as you can and drop the objects down on to the tray. (Try to let go of both objects at the same time.) Listen for the sound of them hitting the tray. Which one lands first?

How it works
You should find that they land together. Gravity pulls them down to Earth at the same speed even though one is heavier than the other.

More things to try
Use different pairs of objects to test the theory. For example: a light, sponge ball and a tennis ball or a cube of sugar and a dice. Choose objects that are the same size and shape but different weights.

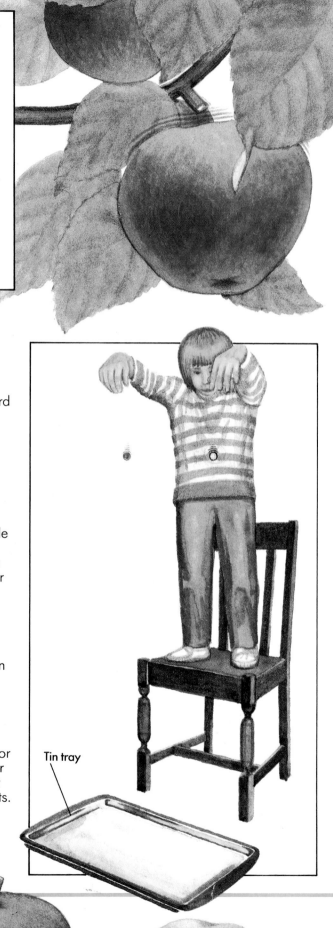

Tin tray

Hitting the Ground

Equipment: Soft modelling clay, a marble or ball bearing, ruler, metal tray.

When objects fall, they hit the ground with a thud! The further objects fall, the bigger the thud. Test this for yourself.

1. Make your modelling clay into a thick, flat pancake shape and put it on to the metal tray.

2. Drop the ball bearing or marble into the modelling clay from different heights. Try 30 cm (1 foot), 60 cm (2 feet) and so on.

3. Measure the size of the dent in the modelling clay each time.

4. Make a chart of your results. What happens as you drop the object from greater heights?

How it works
Objects that fall from a greater height are travelling faster when they hit the ground than objects that fall only a short distance. So the object dropped from the highest point makes the largest dent in the modelling clay. Objects dent the ground if it is softer than they are. But soft objects can be damaged if they hit a hard surface. Think about a soft peach falling from a shopping bag!

Falling Coins

Place a ruler on the edge of a table so one end just sticks out over the edge and the other end is about 3 cm (1 inch) from the edge. Place two identical coins in the positions shown in the diagram. Use another ruler to hit the ruler on the table and watch carefully to see which coin hits the ground first. (You may have to do this several times.)

How it works
Both coins hit the ground at the same time despite the fact that they take different paths. The coin on the end of the ruler simply falls straight down under the pull of gravity when you hit the ruler from under it. The other coin is knocked off the table by the ruler. Because it is given a push it travels more quickly than the first coin so it catches up and the two coins hit the ground together.

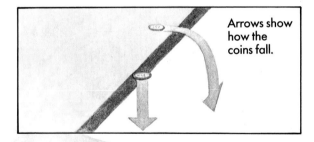

Arrows show how the coins fall.

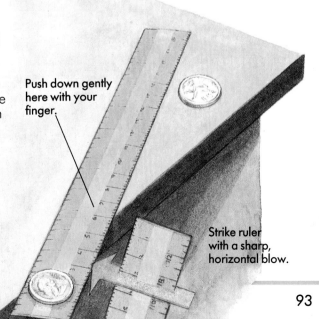

Push down gently here with your finger.

Strike ruler with a sharp, horizontal blow.

Gravity and Weight

Objects have weight because gravity pulls on them. The greater the pull of gravity on an object, the more it weighs.

Make a Spring Balance

This spring balance will help you to compare the weight of small objects.

Equipment: A yoghurt pot, thin string, paperclips, a small nail or drawing pin, paper, ruler, pencils, elastic band.

1. Hammer the nail or press the drawing pin into a vertical surface from which you can hang the balance.

Floating in Space

People do not feel their weight if there is no gravity pulling on them or if they are floating freely. When you bounce on a trampoline you feel weightless when you are up in the air but the feeling will last only until you come down to Earth again.

The pull of the Earth's gravity gets less further out in space so things weigh less in space. Astronauts float about in their spacecraft because there is little gravity to pull them down.

▶ Astronaut Irwin on the Moon during the Apollo 15 Mission. Gravity on the Moon is about one-sixth of the gravity on Earth so a spacesuit that weighs 83 kilograms (183 pounds) on Earth weighs only 14 kilograms (31 lbs) on the Moon. This makes it much easier for astronauts to move about on the Moon; they can even hop around like kangaroos!

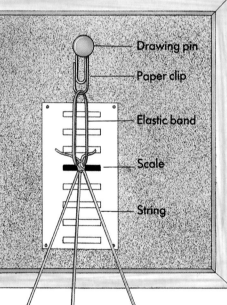

2. Loop the elastic band inside the paper clip and hang the paper clip from the nail or drawing pin.
3. Make three holes in the rim of the yoghurt pot and thread the string through them to make a handle. Tie the ends together and then tie them on to the end of the elastic band.
4. Make a scale for your balance using a piece of paper or card fixed behind the elastic band. Mark the point at the end of the elastic band before you weigh something and then mark how far down this point comes when you have something in the pot.

Drawing pin

Paper clip

Elastic band

Scale

String

Compare the weight of small objects such as pencils, a marble, a stone, a handkerchief or a few grapes.

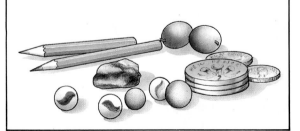

Moving the Oceans

Tides in the oceans on Earth are caused by the pull of the gravity of the Moon and the Sun. Because the Moon is closer to the Earth than the Sun, it pulls the oceans more than the Sun. In most parts of the world, the sea level rises about twice a day (high tides) and falls in between (low tides).

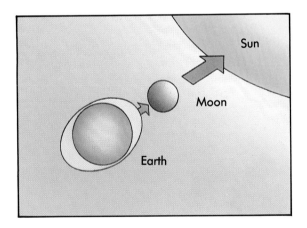

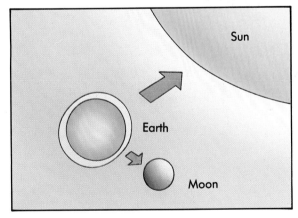

When the Sun is in line with the Moon and the Earth their forces of gravity pull together. This pull makes the tides very high in the part of the Earth closest to the Moon. These high tides are called **spring tides**. They usually occur about every two weeks, at the time of a full Moon and a new Moon.

When the Sun and Moon are at right angles to each other, their pull is weaker and causes much smaller tides on the Earth. These are called **neap tides**. If you live near the sea, you should be able to find out when the spring and neap tides occur in your area.

Balancing

Rest a book on the edge of a table, and gradually ease it over the edge. It will balance with part of the book off the table until you push it too far and upset the balance. All objects have a point where they are held in balance by the force of gravity. This balancing point is called the **centre of gravity** because it is the place where the whole weight of the objects seems to centre.

Find the Balancing Point

The balancing point of a regular shape, such as a square or a circle, is in the centre. This experiment will show you how to find the balancing points of more irregular shapes. All you need is card, string, a weight and a pin or nail.

Cut out an irregular shape from the card and make three holes in the edge. Tie the weight to the string. When you hold up the string, the weight will make it hang straight down in a vertical line. This is called a **plumb line**.

Hang your shape and the plumb line on a pin or nail and draw a straight line down the string. Do the same thing with the other two holes. The balancing point is where the three lines cross.

More things to try

Draw and cut out a boat shape and find the balancing point. Then tape a weight in different places on the boat. How does the weight change the balancing point? Where do you think is the best place for the cargo to be stowed on a real ship?

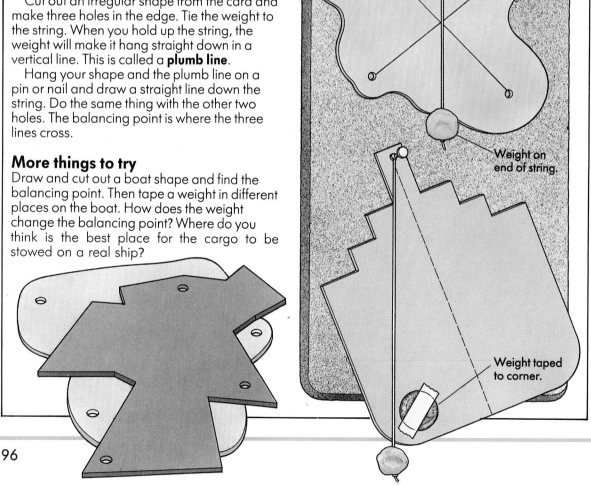

Lines cross at centre.

Weight on end of string.

Weight taped to corner.

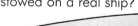

The Magic Box

A box is a regular shape so you would expect the balancing point to be in the middle. This trick will show you how to defy the laws of balancing and surprise your friends. You need a small box and a heavy weight.

Tape the weight into one corner of the box. Then put on the lid and show it to your friends. Open the lid away from the weight and let them see the box looks empty. (You could make a false bottom for the box to hide the weight.) Tell them that the box is magic and you can balance it on air. Then place the box on a table and gradually ease it off the edge. If you leave the corner with the weight in it on the table, the rest of the box will hang in the air as if by magic!

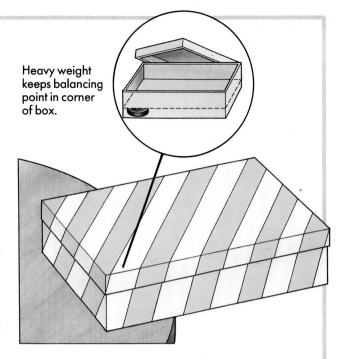

Heavy weight keeps balancing point in corner of box.

Make a Candle See-Saw

Equipment: A metal tray, two cans, two thin nails or pins, a long candle.

1. Scrape away some wax from the flat end of the candle so the wick pokes through and you can light it at both ends.
2. Measure the candle to find the middle and push in the two nails, one on each side.
3. Rest the nails on the cans to make a see-saw.
4. Place the see-saw on the tray and check that it balances. Then light both ends.

How it works
Before the candle is lit, the balancing point is in the middle. When a drop of wax falls from one end, the balancing point moves to the other side and the see-saw tips. If the candle drips first from one end and then the other, the see-saw will go up and down as the balancing point moves from one side to the other.

Warning: Remember to put out the candle when you have finished.

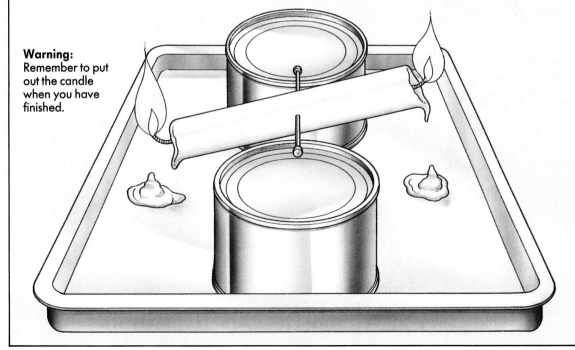

Objects can balance when their centre of gravity allows them to stay upright or poised in position. Here are two balancing toys you can make. They both have their centre of gravity low down so it is hard to make them lose their balance.

Make a Tightrope Walker

Equipment: A small potato, a cocktail stick, two forks, thin wire or strong thread.
1. Fix a small potato on the end of a cocktail stick and attach two forks to the potato as shown in the illustration.
2. Make a notch in the end of the cocktail stick so it will fit better on the tightrope.

Notch in end of cocktail stick.

Make a Gymnast

1. Carefully draw the shape of the gymnast on to the card or paper.
2. Cut out two shapes exactly the same. One will be the front of your gymnast and the other will be the back. Give your figure a colourful costume.
3. Fix one coin behind each hand using sticky tape. Then stick the two halves of the figure together.
4. When your gymnast is dry, it will balance on its nose almost anywhere. Try balancing it on your finger, the rim of a glass or a piece of string stretched tightly.

How it works
Although the figure looks heavier at the top, the weight of the coins keeps the centre of gravity under the nose so it will balance.

Equipment: Thin card or thick paper, scissors, two small coins (the same weight), glue, sticky tape.

Tape coins to back of hands.

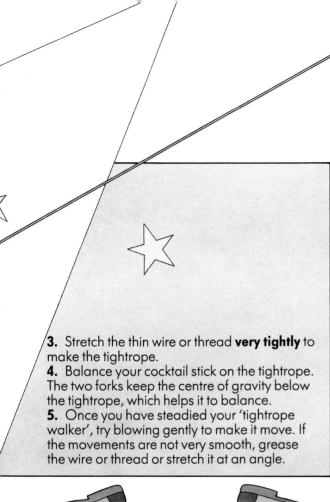

3. Stretch the thin wire or thread **very tightly** to make the tightrope.
4. Balance your cocktail stick on the tightrope. The two forks keep the centre of gravity below the tightrope, which helps it to balance.
5. Once you have steadied your 'tightrope walker', try blowing gently to make it move. If the movements are not very smooth, grease the wire or thread or stretch it at an angle.

See-Saws

Two people who weigh about the same can balance if they sit on either end of a see-saw. But what happens if one person is much heavier than the other? Try this investigation to find out how to make the see-saw balance.

1. Cut the tube in half, place it flat side down and balance the ruler across it.
2. Put one coin at each end – they balance because the centre of gravity is in the middle.
3. Add a second coin to one end. This makes the heavier end lower but can you make the see-saw balance again without adding any more weights?
4. Move the pile of two coins closer to the middle of the ruler until the see-saw balances again. You should find that the see-saw will balance when the two coins are halfway between the centre and the end of the ruler. This is because they are twice as heavy as the load at the lighter end. Can you think of another way to make the see-saw balance?

Equipment: A 30 cm (1 foot) ruler, several coins of the same size, a cardboard tube.

▲ A heavy person has to sit nearer to the middle of a see-saw to balance a lighter person at the other end.

Start and Stop

Objects that are still do not want to move and objects that are moving do not want to stop. This tendency of something to stay still or keep moving is called **inertia**. (The word comes from the Latin word for 'lazy'.) To make something start or stop moving, you must overcome its inertia. You can do this by pushing or pulling the object. These pushes and pulls are known as **forces**. The heavier something is the more force it needs to start or stop it moving.

Getting Things Moving

Is it easier to start something moving quickly or slowly? Try this experiment to find out.

1. Tie a length of cotton around two heavy books.
2. Rest a board across two empty cans and put the books on top.
3. Gently pull the cotton. The books should start moving quite easily.
4. Now keep the cotton slack and give it a really hard tug. This time the cotton should break because the books have too much inertia to start moving quickly.

Does it need more pulling power to start an object moving . . . or to keep it going?

All you need is a toy car and an elastic band. First try pulling the elastic band. Notice that the harder you pull, the longer it becomes. Then fix the elastic band to the front of the car and pull the car along. You will find that you have to pull quite hard to start the car moving but it needs less pull to keep it going.

Pull gently

Tug really hard

Longer band means you are pulling harder.

Spinning Egg Puzzle

How can you tell the difference between a raw egg and a cooked egg without breaking them? Inertia can help you to solve this puzzle.

Spin each egg in turn on a plate. The egg that keeps spinning for longer is the cooked one. Now spin the eggs again but quickly stop them spinning. Then immediately let them both go again. The cooked egg will stay still but the raw egg will start spinning again.

How it works
The contents of the egg have more inertia when they are liquid (in the raw egg) than when they are solid (in the cooked egg). This slows the raw egg down so it stops spinning before the cooked egg. But when you stopped the eggs and then let go, the liquid in the raw egg was still moving. This movement started the egg spinning again.

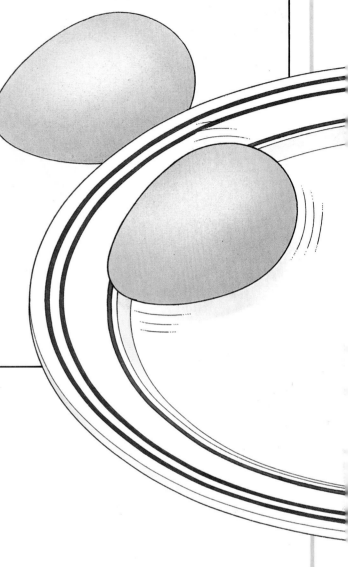

Next time you are in a car, notice what happens if the driver pulls away suddenly. Your inertia pushes you back into your seat – you are not moving and your body wants to stay still. If the driver stops suddenly, you will continue forward as your inertia resists stopping – your body does not want to stop moving.

Seat belts help to overcome your inertia and hold you firmly in your seat. The photographs to the left show dummies being used to test seat belts at a road research centre. The dummy in the top picture is wearing a seat belt; the one in the bottom picture is not.

The Lazy Coin

Equipment: A glass, a piece of card, a coin.

Balance the card across the top of the glass and balance the coin in the middle of the card. Can you make the coin fall straight down into the glass without touching the coin?

How it works
Once again you can use inertia to make this trick work. If you flick the card forwards, the coin has too much inertia to move and should fall neatly into the glass.

More things to try
- Balance the coin on top of the card on the edge of the glass.
- Use a marble instead of a coin. You will need to put a little sugar or a sponge in the glass to stop the marble breaking the glass.
- Balance a cooked egg on the edge of the outside of a matchbox and put it in the middle of the card. (You will need sugar or a sponge in the glass again.) Only the egg has enough inertia to stay still and so it falls into the glass.

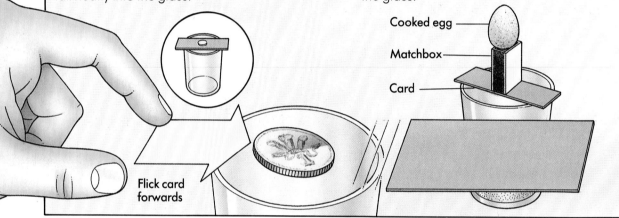

Flick card forwards

Cooked egg

Matchbox

Card

The Tablecloth Trick

You may have seen a magician pull away a tablecloth but leave the cups and saucers safe and sound on the table. This is not a good trick for you to try at home so here is another version that will not do any damage if it goes wrong! All you need is a small sheet of paper and a plastic mug of water (try a glass or an **old** cup and saucer when you have perfected the trick).

Stand the mug of water on the paper on a table. Make sure the outside of the mug is completely dry – the trick will not work if it is wet. Can you pull out the paper without spilling the water in the mug?

How it works
If you pull the paper with a sharp jerk, the mug should stay where it is. (Do not lift the paper; keep it flat on the table.) The mug has too much inertia to be moved by the sudden jerk.

Demolish the Tower

Make a tower out of draughts on a flat table. Can you take the tower down one layer at a time without touching it?

Line up the ruler with the bottom draught in the pile. Leave the end of the ruler hanging over the edge of the table. Then push the ruler towards the tower with a sharp tap or swing it sideways under the tower. As it hits the bottom draught, it should push it out of the way but leave the rest of the tower standing. With practice, you should be able to remove the draughts one by one.

How it works
The tower has a large inertia and the small, sharp push at the bottom is not enough to overcome this inertia and make the whole tower move.

Sliding Along

One way of moving things is to slide them over another surface. Think about pulling a sledge. Does it slide more easily on ice or on a concrete path? When two rough or uneven surfaces rub together an invisible force called **friction** holds them back and makes moving difficult. Moving is easier when there is little friction between two surfaces.

▶ Smooth or even surfaces produce less friction. That is why it is easy to zoom down a shiny slide in the park.

Investigate Friction

Arrange a selection of objects in a line along the edge of a smooth piece of wood. Then slowly raise the wood until the objects begin to move. Make a note of the objects that move first. Repeat the experiment using a metal tray. Do the objects move more easily . . . or less easily? Do you have to lift the metal tray higher than the wooden board before the objects will move? Which surface has the lowest friction?

How it works
Some of the objects move more easily than others because there is less friction between their outer surface and the surface of the board or tray. Feel the objects that move easily. They should feel smooth.

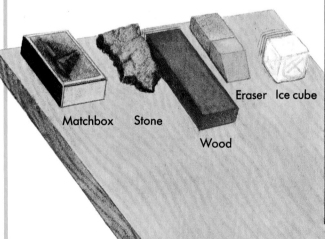

Matchbox   Stone   Eraser   Ice cube

Wood

Friction in Water

Friction does not only hold back objects on solid surfaces. It also makes it more difficult for objects to move in water.

Take a smooth rubber ball and a tennis ball. Put a little water in a shallow bowl. Try spinning each ball in the dish.
Which one moves more easily?

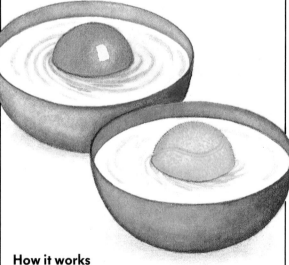

How it works
Once again, the smooth surface causes less friction so the rubber ball moves more easily than the tennis ball. This is why a fast boat has a smooth hull.

Friction Keeps Things Moving

Friction always makes it harder to move things but this can sometimes be very useful. For example, the friction between the soles of your shoes and the ground stops you slipping over when you walk and the wheels of a car could not grip the road without friction. In the illustration below are some examples of how useful friction can be.

The studs on football boots increase friction to stop the players slipping over.

Friction allows the players to kick the ball. Without friction it would slide off their feet.

Friction helps to keep the screws in the wood of the goalposts and stops the knots in the netting from coming undone.

Life Without Friction

Here are some tricks that will show you how difficult life might be without friction.

- Screw on the top of a glass jar as hard as you can. Then wet your hands with soap and water and try to remove the lid. You will find it is impossible! The soap and water reduce the friction so much that you cannot grip the lid well enough to unscrew it.

- Rub a little vaseline or margarine on to the handle of a door (remember to clean it off again afterwards). Then try to turn the handle. Once again you will find you need friction to open the door.

Gloves create friction, which helps the goalkeeper to hold onto the ball.

Increasing Friction

Sometimes it is very useful to increase the amount of friction between things to keep them moving. For example, in icy conditions grit is spread on roads to make the surface rougher, and increase the friction between the tyres and the road. This helps the tyres to grip the road. Tractors and snow-ploughs have tyres with large, deep treads or grooves to produce a lot of friction and give them a good grip on slippery surfaces.

Reducing Friction ...

Smoothing out surfaces helps to reduce friction and make things move more easily. Polishing surfaces helps to keep them smooth. The special floors in bowling alleys are polished for this reason. Water and oil can also be used to reduce friction. They fill in some of the bumps in a surface or form a layer that stops two surfaces from rubbing against one another.

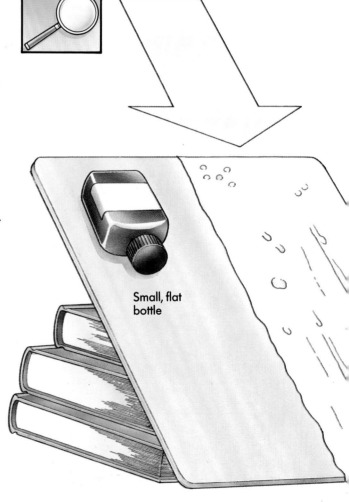

Small, flat bottle

... With Water

Equipment: A smooth metal tray, books, a small flat bottle, water, soap.
1. Prop up the tray on the books to make a slope.
2. Wet one side of the tray and try sliding the bottle down each side in turn.
3. Now rub soap on the wet side and slide the bottle down again. On which surface does the bottle slide most easily?
How it works
There is most friction between the glass and the dry metal of the tray. Even though they feel smooth, there are bumps in the glass and the metal. The water fills in some of the bumps in the surfaces so there is less friction. The soap fills in even more bumps and the bottle slides very easily. In fact the bottle slides on a layer of soapy water, not on the metal. Wet things are slippery because water smooths out the bumps in surfaces. This can be dangerous – it is easy for a car to skid on a wet road.

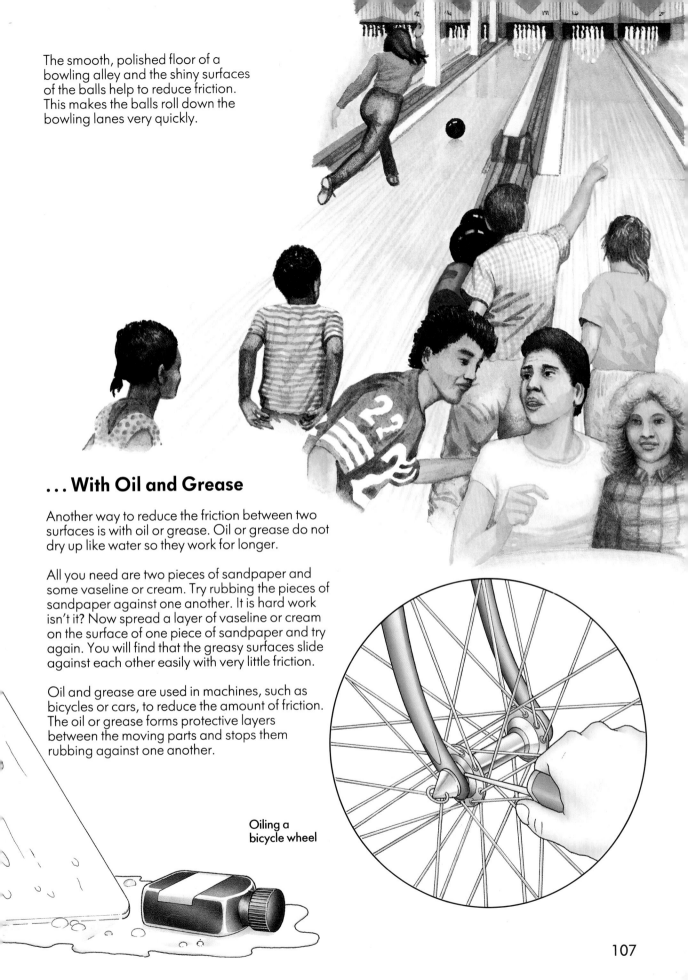

The smooth, polished floor of a bowling alley and the shiny surfaces of the balls help to reduce friction. This makes the balls roll down the bowling lanes very quickly.

. . . With Oil and Grease

Another way to reduce the friction between two surfaces is with oil or grease. Oil or grease do not dry up like water so they work for longer.

All you need are two pieces of sandpaper and some vaseline or cream. Try rubbing the pieces of sandpaper against one another. It is hard work isn't it? Now spread a layer of vaseline or cream on the surface of one piece of sandpaper and try again. You will find that the greasy surfaces slide against each other easily with very little friction.

Oil and grease are used in machines, such as bicycles or cars, to reduce the amount of friction. The oil or grease forms protective layers between the moving parts and stops them rubbing against one another.

Oiling a bicycle wheel

107

Slopes and Rollers

Heavy things are very difficult to move but there are several ways of making them easier to move. You can find out about some of them on the next eight pages.

► In this exit to a multi-storey car park, the vehicles drive down a slope that winds round and round. This allows them to descend easily from a great height within a small space.

Investigate Slopes

Make a loop out of the string and tie it to the toy. Put your finger through the loop and try to lift the toy to a height of about 60 cm (2 feet). You will find it is hard work!

Then use the plank to make a slope up to the seat of the chair. Put your finger through the loop of string again and pull the toy up the slope. You will find it is easier to pull something up a gentle slope than a steep one.

How many examples can you find of slopes or ramps being used to make it easier to lift things? Look in garages and railway stations.

Equipment: A heavy toy with wheels (such as a roller skate), string, a plank, a chair.

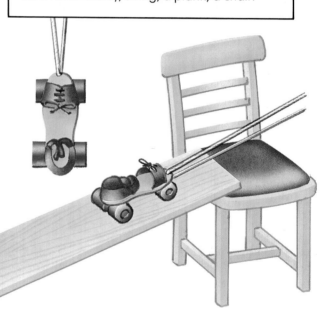

It is easier to move up a gentle slope than to try and climb straight up a steep slope – even though you may travel further. This is why mountain roads often wind round and round. If the road went straight up the mountain the slope would be too steep for cars and trucks to climb.

► The ancient Egyptians used winding slopes to help them build structures such as pyramids. They also used rollers made from tree trunks to help them move the heavy stones they needed to build their monuments.

Rolling Along

It is easier to move a heavy load on rollers rather than slide it along the ground or carry it. Try this experiment to find out why.

Equipment: A metal tray, salt or flour, a tin.

1. Spread out the flour or salt on the tray.
2. Stand the tin on its end and push it along.
3. Then turn the tin on its side and roll it along.

How it works
As you slide the tin along, you push the flour or salt into little heaps and this makes it more difficult to move the tin. Rolling is much easier because you smooth out the flour so there is less friction.

It is possible to roll objects that are not round by putting rollers underneath them.

Take a heavy book and three or four **round** pencils. Try pushing the book along a table. Then balance the book on the pencils and push it along again. It is much easier to move the book if the pencils act as rollers. But you will have to keep putting the back pencil under the front of the book as it moves forward.

Wheels

Wheels make it easier to move things. They are more useful than rollers because they can be fixed to whatever has to be moved. This makes it possible to move a heavy load quickly and easily.

The wheel was invented about 6000 years ago but no one knows who invented it. Perhaps it was someone who had used logs as rollers to help them move things. Wheels are made of all sorts of materials such as wood, plastic, metal or rubber.

Spin the Book

Many of the wheels on fast-moving machines (such as cars and bicycles) have ball bearings inside them. This trick will show you why. Place a circle of marbles in the rim of the tin and balance the book on top. If you push the book gently, you should be able to spin it easily. Try again without the marbles. It can't be done!

How it works
The marbles reduce the friction between the book and the tin so it is possible to spin the book. The ball bearings between a wheel and an axle work in a similar way. In a wheel without ball bearings, the axle and wheel rub together and this slows the wheel down.

Equipment: An empty tin with a rim (such as a syrup or cocoa tin), marbles, a book.

Looking at Gears

Special toothed wheels of different sizes, which are called **gears**, can work together to make things work more quickly or more slowly. Each time a large wheel turns once it can turn a smaller wheel several times. The number of times the smaller wheel turns depends on the number of teeth or 'cogs' each gear wheel has.

Look for gears on machines such as bicycles, clocks or egg beaters. Do the gears speed up or slow down the parts being turned? Notice how the big gear wheel on an egg beater fits into the smaller wheel and count how many times the small wheel turns when you turn the big wheel. (If you mark the wheels with a marker pen you will be able to count the turns more easily. Wash any marks off the beater afterwards.)

Test These Gears

Trace the gear wheels below on to thin card. Push a pin or small nail through the middle of the wheels and fix them to a sheet of cardboard so they will turn round easily. Arrange the smallest and largest wheels so that the cogs meet.

- How many times does the small wheel turn if you turn the big wheel once?
- Do both wheels turn the same way?

Then repeat your experiments with three gear wheels in a row. Try to guess which way the third gear wheel will turn before you try the experiment.

Changing Direction

Gear wheels can also be used to change movement from one direction to another.

Equipment: Two round slices of potato, several cocktail sticks, two long, thin nails.

1. Fix 6 pieces of cocktail stick into the sides of each potato slice.
2. Push one nail through the middle of each slice to act as an axle.
3. Pin one slice up onto a sheet of cardboard or a notice board.
4. Hold the second wheel up by its axle in a horizontal position and use it to turn the vertical wheel.

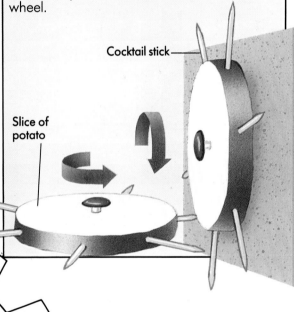

Cocktail stick

Slice of potato

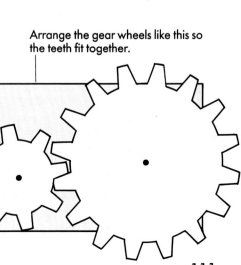

Trace the gear wheels separately, **not** one inside the other.

Arrange the gear wheels like this so the teeth fit together.

111

Pulley Power

Pulleys are a special sort of wheel. A pulley wheel has a groove all round the rim for a rope to fit into. If you attach one end of the rope to a heavy load you will be able to lift it more easily.

Cranes use pulleys and levers (see pages 114–115) to help them lift heavy loads. Count the number of pulleys on the cranes you see. The biggest cranes have three or four pulleys. A motor provides the power to pull the cable over the pulley wheels.

Broom and Rope Trick

Amaze your friends with your super strength using this simple trick. Ask two or four friends to hold two brooms apart. Attach a length of rope to one broom and thread it round the two brooms as shown in the diagram. Take hold of the free end yourself. Ask your friends to try and keep the brooms apart while you try and pull them together. You should find that you are easily able to beat the pulling power of your friends.

Hint: Dust the brooms with talcum powder before you give them to your friends to hold. This will reduce the friction and make it easier for you to pull the brooms together.

Make Your Own Pulleys

1. Bend about 20 cm (8 inches) of wire into a triangle shape and push the ends into the cotton reel. (Ask an adult to help you cut and bend the wire.)
2. Find a suitable place to hang your pulley. A hook in the shed or garage or the hook at the end of a plant hanger will do.
3. Tie one end of the string to the handle of the load.
4. Wind the string over the cotton reel.

● Is it easier to lift the load with the pulley?
● How much string do you have to use to lift the load 30 cm (1 foot)?

Now try a double pulley...
1. Make two wire triangles. Use about 35 cm (1 foot 2 inches) of wire for each one.
2. Attach two cotton reels to each triangle.
3. Thread the string round the pulleys as shown in the diagram. Use about 2 metres (6½ feet) of string.
4. Attach the heavy load to the pulley as before.

Equipment: Wire, cotton reels, string, a hook, toy bucket full of heavy objects.

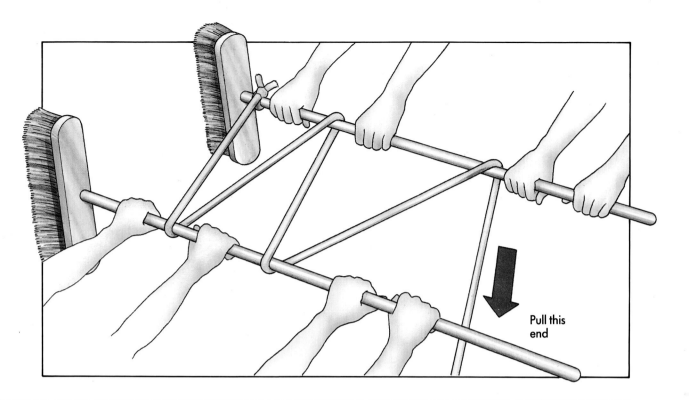

Pull this
end

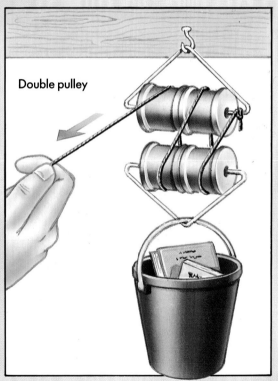

Double pulley

- Is it easier to lift the load with the double pulley?
- How much string do you need to raise the load 30 cm (1 foot)?

How it works

The pulley with one cotton reel allows you to lift a heavy load directly underneath the pulley. The double pulley means you use only a quarter of the pull but you need four times the amount of string.

Levers and Lifting

One of the simplest ways of lifting heavy things more easily is to use a lever. Levers work by increasing the pushing force underneath the object so a large load can be moved with a small effort. Levers lift objects most easily when the resting point – the **'fulcrum'** – is close to the object and the pushing point is as far away as possible.

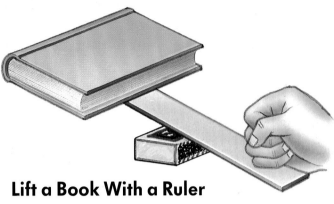

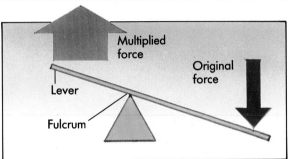

Lift a Book With a Ruler

Choose a heavy book. Lift it up and notice how heavy it is. Make a lever using a ruler balanced across a matchbox. Make sure that the fulcrum (the place where the ruler rests across the matchbox) is close to one end of the ruler. Place the book on the end of the ruler nearest to the fulcrum. You will find that you will be able to lift the book easily by pressing down gently on the other end of the ruler. Notice how far down you have to push the ruler and how high the book is lifted.

Jumping Coin Trick

Equipment: A ruler, a pencil, two large coins.

Use this trick to find out where to push on a lever to get the best lift.

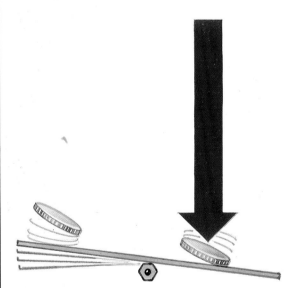

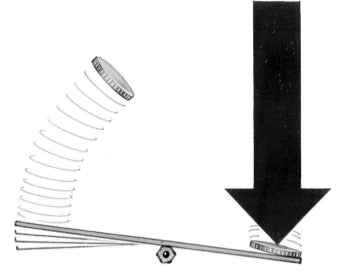

1. Put the pencil under the middle of the ruler and place a coin on one end. Drop the second coin from a height of about 30 cm (1 foot) so it hits the ruler at about the 7.5 cm (3 inch) mark. Notice how high the first coin jumps into the air.

2. Now repeat the trick but drop the second coin right at the end of the ruler. (Be sure to drop it from the same height.) You should see that the first coin jumps much higher into the air this time.

Hit the Boundary

You may be surprised to learn that your arm is a lever too. Throw a ball into the air and hit it with your hand. Then try hitting the ball with a bat. You will find that you can hit the ball with a much greater force using the bat. Your arm is working as a lever with your elbow as the fulcrum. Your muscles provide the pushing force. When you use a bat, the hitting point is further from your elbow (the fulcrum) so the pushing force is greater and you might reach the boundary with your hit!

Acrobats use the same idea in their tricks. The acrobat who is to spring off the see-saw stands close to the fulcrum. The acrobat who jumps onto the see-saw to catapult his partner jumps as far away from the fulcrum as possible to give the greatest possible lift.

How it works

The coin hits the ruler with the same force because you dropped it from the same height. The coin jumped higher the second time because the lever (the ruler) has more lifting power when the pushing force is further away from the fulcrum.

More things to try

- Try prising the lid from a tin. Is it easier with a short lever or a long lever?
- Where is the best place for a light person to sit on a see-saw in order to lift a heavy person?

115

Investigating Pendulums

Equipment: String and some weights, a hook, a watch with a second hand.

Cut two lengths of string – make each one about 1 metre (3 feet) long. Tie a small weight to one piece of string and a larger weight to the other piece. Tie each pendulum in turn to a hook or somewhere where it can swing freely. Set the pendulum swinging gently and time how long it takes to swing to and fro ten times. You will find that both pendulums take the same amount of time to complete ten swings even though they have different weights on the end.

Then try some experiments with one weight. First attach it to a long string. How long do ten swings take? Then try again with a shorter string. You will find that the pendulum with the shorter string swings much faster than the one with the longer string.

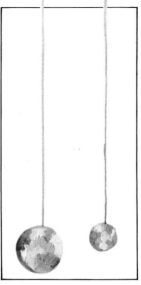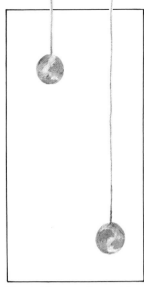

Large weight   Small weight   Short string   Long string

▶ Pendulums are used in clocks. They swing to and fro at a fixed rate so they make the clockwork mechanism move at a steady speed.

Swinging

On the next eight pages you can find out about different sorts of movement, such as swinging, twisting, stretching and spinning. On these two pages you can discover more about swinging by looking at how pendulums work. A pendulum is a rod or string with a weight called a 'bob' on the end. In the 16th century Galileo noticed that the chandelier in the cathedral at Pisa took the same time to complete one swing whether the swing was a long one or a short one. He also found that the time of the swing depended on the length of the pendulum – the weight on the end made no difference. Try this yourself.

Shifting Pendulums

One pendulum can set another swinging. Here is how it works.

Equipment: Modelling clay, string, two chairs, heavy books (optional).

Cut two pieces of string about 45 cm (1½ feet) long and attach a piece of modelling clay to each piece of string. Tie some string tightly between the backs of two chairs and put some books on the chairs to hold them steady (or ask someone to hold the chairs). Tie the pendulums to the line of string. Hold one pendulum still and start the other swinging. What happens when you let go of the second pendulum?

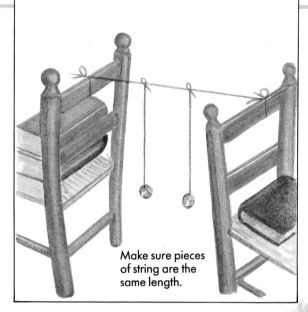

Make sure pieces of string are the same length.

Pendulum Skittles

This is an outdoor game of skill that you can make very easily.

Equipment: A ball about the size of a tennis ball, string, a flat board or flat surface, pencils and cotton reels (or empty, plastic lemonade bottles).

1. Fix about 1.5 metres (5 feet) of string to the ball.
2. Hang the ball from a suitable tree branch or other overhanging bar so it swings about 15 cm (6 inches) above the ground.
3. Make skittles by standing pencils in the middle of the cotton reels.
4. Set up the skittles on the board or on the ground if it is flat.

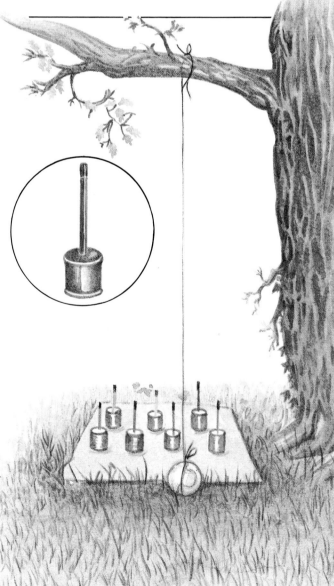

Rules
Swing the pendulum so it does **not** hit the skittles on the outward swing but knocks them over on the return swing. This will take some practice! You can make the game more interesting by giving each skittle different points and keeping the score.

Stretch and Twist

What makes a ball bounce or a catapult spring? Some substances, such as elastic or rubber, stretch when you pull them but spring back to their original shape and size when you let them go. You can use this springy energy to have fun!

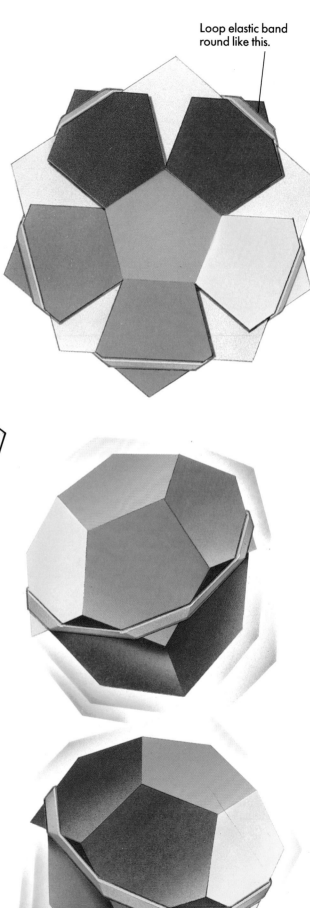

Loop elastic band round like this.

Jumping Monsters

Equipment: Thin card, coloured pencils, a long elastic band, scissors.

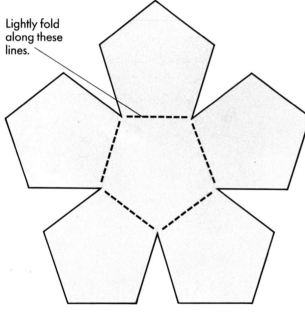

Lightly fold along these lines.

1. Draw a five-sided shape like this onto the thin card. Lightly fold back where shown by the dotted lines.

2. Cut out the shape and then make another one exactly the same.

3. Decorate your monster with patterns or faces.

4. Overlap the two shapes and loop the elastic band over every other corner to hold the two halves of your monster together. Make sure the elastic is slightly stretched but not too tight.

5. When you let go of the monster it will jump up into a solid shape.

How it works

The energy in the stretched elastic band pulls the cardboard into the monster shape.

Magic Rolling Tin

Equipment: A large tin with a lid, a hammer and nail to make holes, an elastic band, a heavy nut or other weight, string.

Ask an adult to help you make two holes in the lid and two holes in the end of the tin using the hammer and nail.

1. Cut the elastic band so you have one long piece.
2. Thread the band through the holes in the tin so it crosses over in the middle. Knot the ends of the elastic band together at the lid end.
3. Tie on the weight inside the can.
4. Press on the lid and roll the tin forward. What happens?

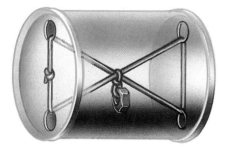

How it works
You will find you have made an obedient tin, which always comes back to you! This is because the heavy weight stays hanging below the elastic band so the elastic becomes twisted. (Don't push the tin too hard or the weight will spin too.) The tin rolls back on its own because it is driven along by the energy stored up in the twisted rubber.

Shrinking Rubber

Weight-lifting is a good trick to try using an elastic band. Most materials expand (get bigger) when they are heated but rubber does the opposite.
1. Cut an elastic band to make one long piece and tie one end on to a toy car or similar weight.
2. Hang the elastic band on a hook so the weight is just resting on a table or other surface.
3. Heat the elastic band by blowing hot air from a hair drier on to it, moving the drier up and down a few times. You will see that the weight is lifted a little way off the table.

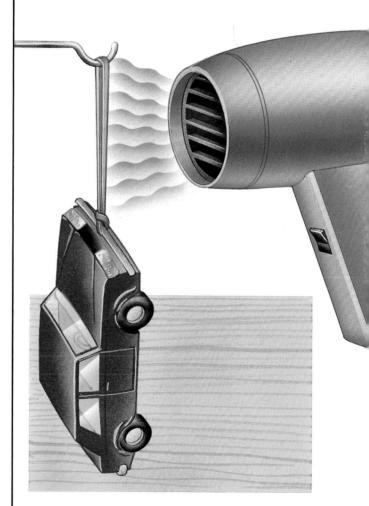

How it works
The heat makes the elastic band contract (get shorter) for a little while so it pulls the weight off the table. But look at the elastic band afterwards. Does it go back to its original size?

Make a Creeping Crawler

Equipment: A cotton reel, a small elastic band, matchsticks, a candle, sticky tape, pencil, scissors or penknife.

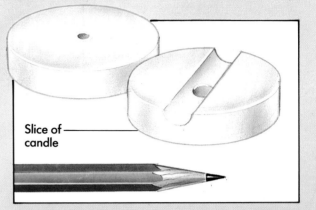

Slice of candle

1. Cut a slice about 10 mm (½ inch) thick from the candle. Make a hole through the middle (where the wick was) using a sharp pencil.
2. Make a groove in one side of the slice using a pencil point or penknife.
3. Push the elastic band through the hole in the slice and place a matchstick through the loop. Pull the elastic band tight so the matchstick fits into the groove.
4. Thread the other end of the elastic band through the hole in the cotton reel.
5. Push half a matchstick through the loop of the elastic band that comes through the reel. Tape the loop and half matchstick firmly to the end of the cotton reel so they cannot turn round.
6. Now wind up your toy by turning the long matchstick (at the candle end) round and round. When you put it down, the toy will start to crawl. You can scare your friends by slipping the toy under a tissue or napkin and making it move as if by magic!

How it works
As you turn the matchstick, you twist and tighten the elastic band. As the band unwinds, it releases the energy stored in the twisted elastic and makes the toy move.

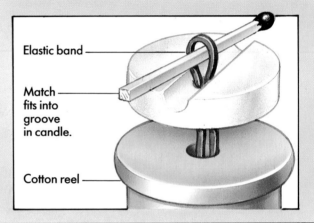

Elastic band

Match fits into groove in candle.

Cotton reel

Dashing Darts

Equipment: A piece of balsa wood or thick polystyrene, two large hooks, two small hooks, an elastic band, beads, a short piece of wire, a propeller (from an old toy or a shop that sells equipment to make models).

1. Shape the balsa wood or polystyrene to make a dart shape.
2. Fix the two large hooks into the top of the dart and two smaller hooks into the bottom.
3. Bend the wire to make a hook at one end. Thread the beads and the propeller over the other end.
4. Attach one end of the elastic band to the front hook in the bottom of the dart and the other end to the hook in the wire. Rest the wire on the other hook in the bottom of the dart.
5. Hang the dart from a piece of string that is pulled very tightly. Twist the elastic band by turning the propeller and let the dart go!

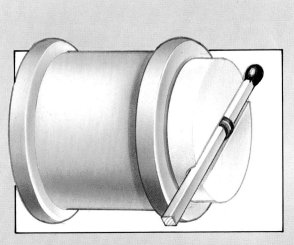

Make a Roundabout

Equipment: The same materials as for the creeping crawler plus a long, thin stick, some thin card and a piece of cotton.

Make the crawler toy as before but fix the thin stick at the candle end instead of the matchstick. Make a small horse or plane out of the card and tie it on to the end of the thin stick using the cotton. Turn the long stick several times to wind up the toy and then stand the cotton reel upright. You may find it easier to press the cotton reel into a piece of modelling clay to stop it wobbling.

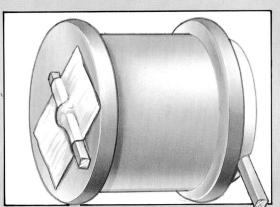

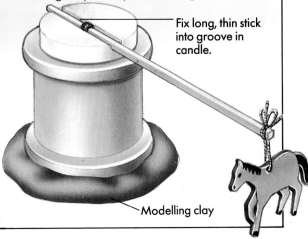

Fix long, thin stick into groove in candle.

Modelling clay

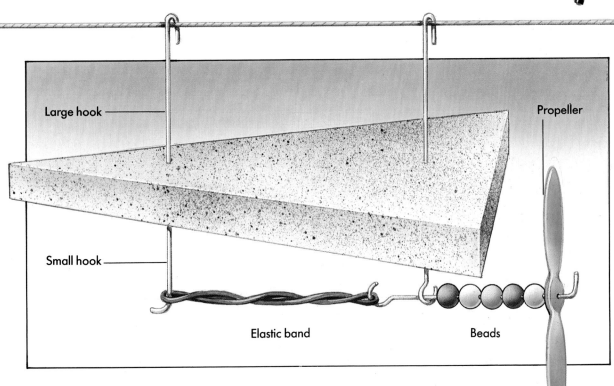

Large hook

Small hook

Elastic band

Beads

Propeller

In a Spin

When an object spins round, it creates a force called **centrifugal force**, which pulls it outwards. You can feel this force if you attach a piece of string to a ball and whirl it round and round in a circle. Centrifugal force is used in the machines at fairgrounds and to spin clothes dry. It even keeps satellites in orbit around the Earth.

Pick up the Marble

Place a marble on a table and cover it with a glass jar. This trick will show you how to lift the marble without touching it.

▼ The 'fly on the wall' ride at fairgrounds works using centrifugal force. The chamber in which the people stand spins round and centrifugal force presses them against the walls. The floor can be lowered leaving them 'stuck' to the walls.

If you spin the jar around, this will start the marble spinning too. Eventually it will be pressed against the sides of the jar by centrifugal force. The mouth of the jar is narrower than the sides so the marble cannot fly out if you lift the jar.

Spinning Water

Spinning forces affect water too. Take a small bucket of water outside and try spinning it round in a circle quite quickly. Centrifugal force will keep the water pressed against the bottom and sides of the bucket while it spins round. This means the water will not fall out of the bucket even when it is upside down!

Make a Spin Drier

Try this investigation to see what happens to water in a container that is spun horizontally and find out how this can be useful.

1. Make three small holes in the rim of the yoghurt pot and use the string to hang the pot from the turning part of the drill or beater.
2. Put about 3 cm (1 inch) of water in the pot. You might like to colour the water with a little food colouring so you can watch it more easily.
3. Turn the handle of the drill or beater steadily so the pot spins round and round. If you watch the water, you will see it pulled against the sides of the pot by centrifugal force.

Equipment: A hand drill or egg beater, thin string, yoghurt pot, water, food colouring.

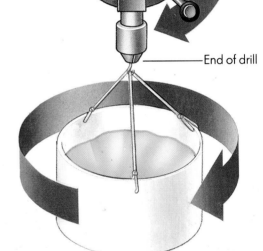

End of drill

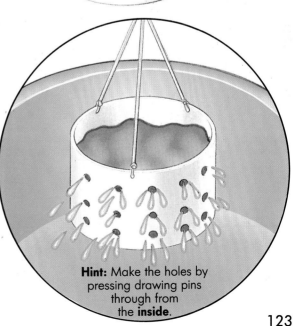

The water is pushed against the sides of the pot.

More things to try

Make holes in the sides of the yoghurt pot and put a very wet piece of cloth inside instead of the water. Spin the pot outdoors or inside a very wide bucket or bowl. You will see that the water in the cloth is thrown out of the pot by centrifugal force. This is just how a real spin drier works. The tub is full of holes and the water in the clothes is pushed out of the holes by centrifugal force as a motor makes the tub spin round.

Hint: Make the holes by pressing drawing pins through from the **inside**.

Machines and Movement

People use a variety of machines to make moving easier. The power to drive these machines comes from animals, which pull carts, ploughs and sledges and also from natural forces, such as the wind and running water. Windmills and water-mills have been used for thousands of years. Today most machines are driven by electricity.

Windmills

People use the pushing power of the wind to drive machines. Windmills have been in use for centuries and are still a common sight today in some parts of the world, such as Holland and Greece. The blades of a windmill are shaped to catch the wind and turn easily. As the blades turn, they make wheels move round to turn grindstones or make other machinery work. Today, scientists are trying out windmills designed to produce electricity.

▶ The blades on this modern experimental windmill are a special shape to help them catch the wind blowing from any direction.

Looking at Water Wheels

There are two main types of water wheel. **Undershot wheels** are moved round by the flow of water as it pushes against the flat paddles sticking out from the wheel.

Undershot wheel

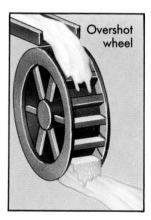

Overshot wheel

Overshot wheels have bucket-shaped paddles to catch the water. The weight of the water in the paddles helps to turn the wheel faster than the weight of the flowing water alone. This wheel needs a difference in the level of the water.

Make a Water Wheel

You can get a good idea of how a water wheel works by making this model and using flowing water from a tap to make it turn round.

1. Cut four pieces of thin card about 3½ cm × 2 cm (1½ inches × 1 inch).
2. Fold each 'blade' in half and glue half of it onto the cotton reel.
3. Push the pencil or knitting needle through the hole in the middle of the cotton reel and hold it under a gently running tap. The force of the water will turn your 'water wheel' round.

Fold here

Equipment: A cotton reel, a long, **round** pencil or knitting needle, card, scissors, glue.

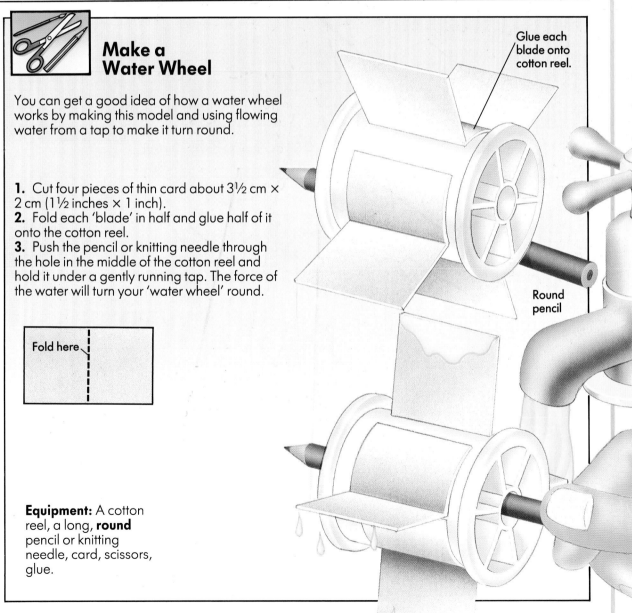

Glue each blade onto cotton reel.

Round pencil

Steam Engines

The power of steam can also be used to make machines move. Over a hundred years ago, the first steam engines were being used to pull railway coaches and to drive the wheels that turned the machinery in mills and factories. Steam engines are still used in some parts of the world today but many have been replaced by engines powered by diesel or electricity.

▲ A steam train on the island of Java, Indonesia. Steam engines have to be kept filled up with water. They pull a trailer called a tender behind them to carry coal or wood for the fire and water to top up the boiler.

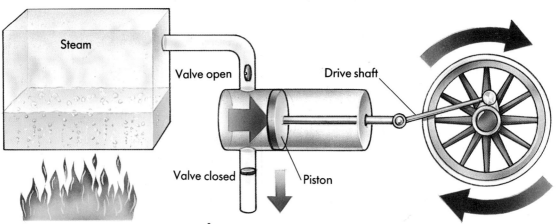

Steam

Valve open

Drive shaft

Valve closed

Piston

How a Steam Engine Works

A steam engine turns heat into mechanical energy, which makes things move. The engine burns coal, oil, or wood to heat water until it turns into steam. The steam takes up more space than the water and pressure builds up.

The pressure of the steam pushes pistons inside metal cylinders. The pistons push a drive shaft, which turns a wheel. The wheel may either move the engine forward or it may turn other engine parts, which drive factory machinery.

Make a Steam Boat

1. Place the three candles inside the tin.
2. Pour about 2 cm (¾ inch) of water into the metal tube. Ask an adult to help you make a small hole in the screw cap of the tube and put the cap on the tube.
3. Use modelling clay to fix the metal tube inside the sardine tin, over the candles.
4. Put the steam boat in the bath or in a pool of water where there is plenty of space.
5. Light the candles and watch the boat travel.

Warning: Make sure you blow out the match and the candles afterwards.

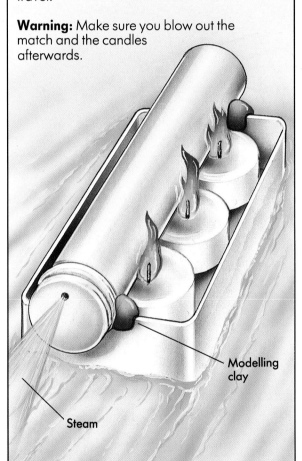

Modelling clay

Steam

Equipment: A clean sardine tin, three thin slices of candle, water, a hollow **metal** tube (such as the one used to hold some indigestion tablets), modelling clay.

How it works
As the candles heat the water in the tube, it boils and turns to steam. The steam shoots out of the hole in the tube and pushes the boat forward.

Turning Turbines

A turbine is a wheel that is turned by the force of water, steam or gas. The wheel has hundreds of metal blades on a long axle. Turbines are used in power stations to provide the energy that turns the generators which produce electricity. They are also used to drive ships and submarines.

In about two-thirds of the world's power stations, strong jets of steam drive the turbine wheels around. In most other power stations, the power of flowing water is used to turn turbines and provide what is called 'hydroelectric power' – 'hydro' means 'to do with water'.

▼ Engineers testing a set of turbines before they are fitted into a power station. There are several turbines in the set, which helps to produce the maximum amount of energy from the steam.

Moving Quiz

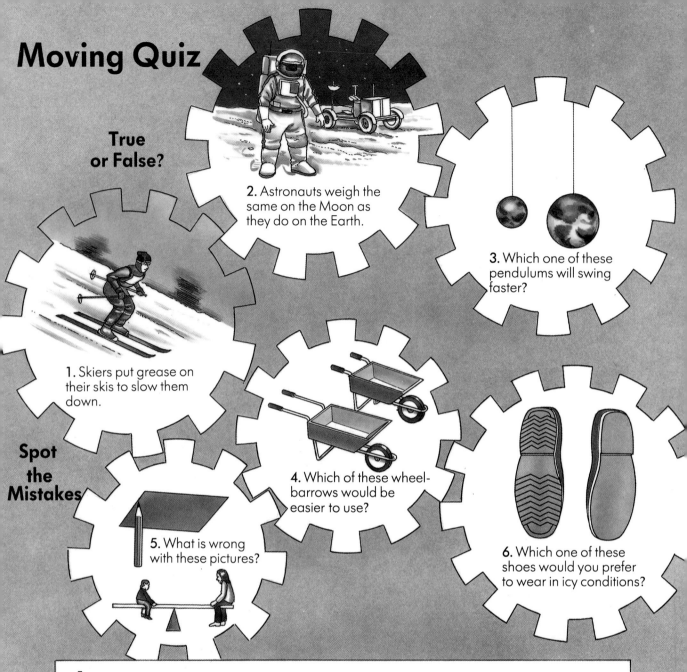

True or False?

2. Astronauts weigh the same on the Moon as they do on the Earth.

3. Which one of these pendulums will swing faster?

1. Skiers put grease on their skis to slow them down.

Spot the Mistakes

4. Which of these wheelbarrows would be easier to use?

5. What is wrong with these pictures?

6. Which one of these shoes would you prefer to wear in icy conditions?

Answers

4. The wheelbarrow with longer handles would be easier to use because the lifting force is further away from the fulcrum or the wheel (page 114).

3. Both pendulums will swing at the same rate. They will complete the same number of swings in one minute (page 116).

2. False. Astronauts weigh about one-sixth of their Earth weight on the Moon (pages 94-95).

1. False. Grease helps to reduce friction and makes the skier travel faster (pages 106-107).

6. The shoe with the ridged sole increases friction so would grip the ice better and make it easier to walk (page 106).

5. Top: Objects with a regular shape have their balancing point or centre of gravity in the centre (page 96).
Bottom: A heavy person has to sit closer to the middle of the see-saw to balance a lighter person on the other end (page 99).

 LIGHT

This section of the book will help you to investigate light. Think about light when you play with the shadows cast by the Sun, or look at yourself in a mirror or when you see a rainbow in the sky.

This section covers six main topics:

- Light and shadows
- Reflection
- Refraction
- Light and sight
- Light and colour
- Light for life; laser light

Use the symbols below to help you identify the three kinds of practical activities in this book.

EXPERIMENTS

TRICKS

THINGS TO MAKE

Introduction

Without light from the Sun, all life on Earth would come to an end. Green plants need Sunlight to make food and you and all the other animals on Earth depend on plants for food.

This book will help you to discover more about Sunlight and the artificial light produced by means of electricity. You can find out why shadows form, how rainbows appear in the sky, how mirrors reflect light and why lenses make things appear to be larger or smaller.

You can also find out about light and colour. Sunlight is made up of several different colours – these are the colours you see in a rainbow. The colour of objects around you depends on which colours they reflect back into your eyes. A special layer at the back of your eyes makes it possible for you to see the world in colour. Understanding how the eye works has helped scientists to develop machines such as microscopes, telescopes, cameras and lasers.

As you carry out the experiments in this book, you will be able to answer the questions on these two pages and come to understand how light and colour influences the world around you.

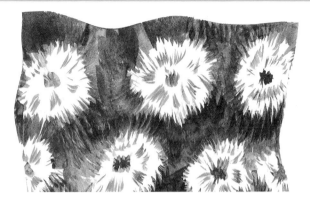

▲ How do you make patterns like this on a piece of cloth? (page 161)

▼ If you spun these discs, what colours would you see? (page 155)

▼ Why do shadows appear behind objects when light shines on them? (pages 132–133)

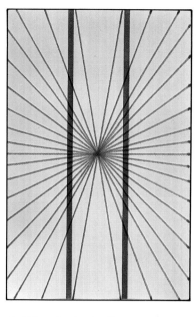

▶ What makes the colours in a rainbow? (pages 154–155)

▲ Why do the red lines appear to be curved, even though they are straight? (page 151)

▼ How does a piece of curved glass make rays of light come closer together? (page 144)

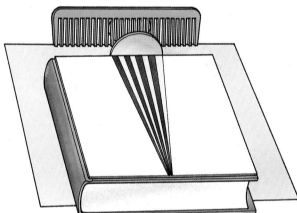

▲ How does a magnifying glass make things look larger? (page 145)

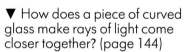

▼ Why can you see reflections in mirrors and other shiny surfaces? (pages 136–137)

▼ Why does grass go yellow if Sunlight cannot reach it? (page 162)

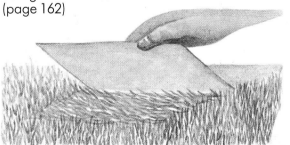

Light and Shadows

Light can pass through some substances, such as glass or water. These are called **transparent** and we can see through them. Other substances, such as paper and metal, stop light passing through. They are called **opaque**. Shadows appear behind opaque substances when light shines on them. Shadows are produced because light travels in straight lines and cannot bend around corners. You can see straight lines of light if you look at the rays of light from the Sun (right).

Shadow Tricks

Shine a torch at a wall in a darkened room. Test a variety of objects and see what sort of shadows they make. See how many different animal shapes you can make using only your hands. You could also draw shadow portraits of your friends or try making up a shadow play using cut-out figures to cast shadows. Cut out an interesting shape (such as a ship, a plane or a clown) from a piece of card and fix it to the end of a stick. Try holding the shape close to the light and then further away. What do you notice about the size of the shadow?

Playing with Shadows

On a sunny day, go outside and investigate shadows with your friends. Try drawing round your shadows on a piece of paper and cutting them out. Does your shadow move when you move? Can you jump on your shadow? Can you shake hands with a friend without your shadows touching? What are the biggest and smallest shadows you can make with your body?

Stand in exactly the same place at different times of day and ask a friend to draw round your shadow with chalk. You will find that the position and shape of your shadow changes as the position of the Sun changes throughout the day. The shadows made by the Sun can be used to tell the time (see pages 134–135).

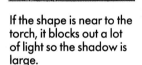

If the shape is near to the torch, it blocks out a lot of light so the shadow is large.

If the shape is further away from the torch, it blocks out less light so the shadow is smaller.

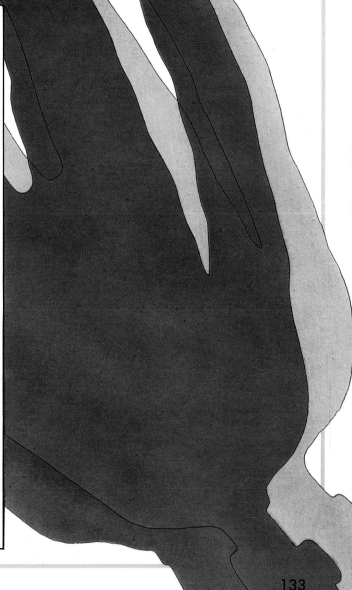

Make a Shadow Clock

Equipment: A long, thin box, pencils, sticky tape, white paper.

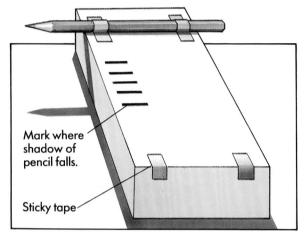

Mark where shadow of pencil falls.

Sticky tape

Cover one side of the box with white paper and hold it in place with sticky tape. Stick a pencil across the end of the box. On a sunny morning, take your shadow clock outside and place it on a pale-coloured, flat surface (such as a sheet of white paper). Point the box in the direction of the Sun. Notice where the shadow of the pencil falls and draw a line at the same point on the top of your box. Write the time next to the line. Do this at several different times during the day. At what time is the end of the shadow nearest to the pencil?

Make a Sundial

Equipment: Thin card, a protractor, a compass, a piece of wood or thick cardboard.

1. On the thin card, draw a right angled triangle. Make the other two angles 45°. The two shorter sides of the triangle should be about 15 cm (6 inches) long. The long side will be a little over 20 cm (8 inches) long.
2. Draw a dotted line as shown in the diagram and cut out the triangle. Fold along the dotted line.
3. Draw a semi-circle on the wood or cardboard as shown in the diagram.
4. Stick the folded part of the triangle firmly to the piece of wood or thick cardboard.
5. Place the sundial in a flat place outside so that the triangle points north-south.
6. Mark the position of the shadow that falls on the base every hour. You should find that the shadow travels the same distance along the semi-circle every hour. On a sunny day you will now be able to tell the time by looking at the position of the shadow on your sundial.

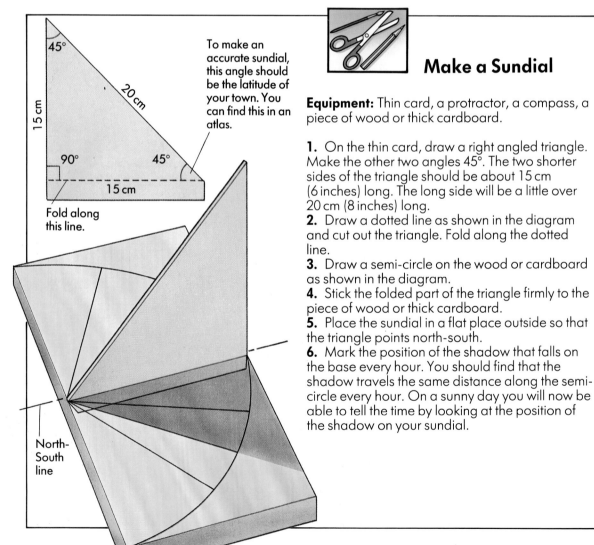

45°

15 cm

20 cm

90°

45°

15 cm

Fold along this line.

To make an accurate sundial, this angle should be the latitude of your town. You can find this in an atlas.

North-South line

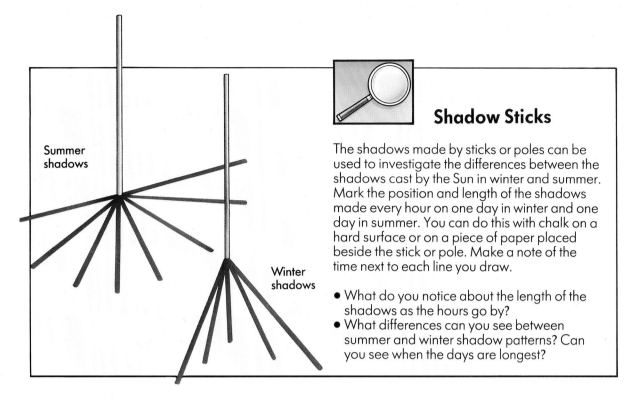

Summer shadows

Winter shadows

Shadow Sticks

The shadows made by sticks or poles can be used to investigate the differences between the shadows cast by the Sun in winter and summer. Mark the position and length of the shadows made every hour on one day in winter and one day in summer. You can do this with chalk on a hard surface or on a piece of paper placed beside the stick or pole. Make a note of the time next to each line you draw.

- What do you notice about the length of the shadows as the hours go by?
- What differences can you see between summer and winter shadow patterns? Can you see when the days are longest?

Shadows in Space

The Moon and the Earth cast their own enormous shadows. When the Moon passes between the Sun and the Earth, its shadow falls on parts of the Earth. This makes these places dark for a time during the day. This is called an **eclipse** of the Sun. When the Earth moves between the Sun and the Moon, it stops Sunlight from reaching the Moon. The Moon becomes dark and this is called an eclipse of the Moon.

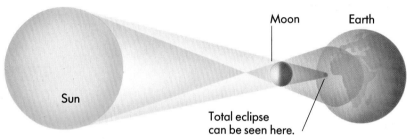

Sun

Moon   Earth

Total eclipse can be seen here.

▶A total eclipse of the Sun. You can see the faint outer atmosphere of the Sun shining out around the black shape of the Moon.

Reflections

When rays of light hit a surface or an object they bounce back off again. This is called **reflection**. Look for reflections in tin foil, cans, bottles and spoons. You will find that flat, shiny surfaces produce the best reflections. This is why most mirrors are made of flat sheets of highly polished glass with a shiny silver coating behind them. Try the experiments on these two pages to find out more about how mirrors reflect light.

Wave at yourself in a mirror with your left hand. Which hand is your reflection using? Mirrors reverse images so that the left side appears to be the right. Ask a friend to pretend to be your reflection and follow your movements for a while.

Investigate Reflections

1. Cut a hole in a piece of the card about 2.5 cm (1 inch) in diameter and tape a comb across the hole.
2. In a darkened room, place the card in front of the torch so that narrow beams of light come through the teeth of the comb.
3. Hold a mirror in the beams of light so that it reflects the light.
4. Move the mirror to a different angle. What happens to the beams of light?

You will see the beams more clearly on a dark surface.

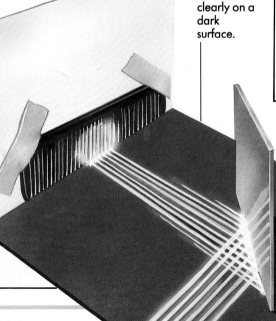

Secret Writing

You can write a secret message to a friend using mirror code. Put a piece of paper in front of a mirror. Look in the mirror and carefully write your message on the paper. When you look at the paper, you will see your message back to front in mirror code. Your friend will be able to decode the message by looking in his or her own mirror.

How it works
Light is reflected off the mirror at exactly the same angle as it hits the mirror. When you change the angle of the mirror, the angle of the reflected light rays changes as well.

More and More Reflections

It is possible to see all round an object if you use more than one mirror. This is because the light rays are bounced from one mirror to the other. Stand two mirrors side by side and put a small object between them. How many reflections can you see?

More things to try
- Move the mirrors closer together and then further apart. What happens to the number of reflections?
- Place two mirrors facing each other with an object between them. You should be able to see endless reflections as the light is bounced to and fro between them.

Make a Kaleidoscope

The patterns inside a kaleidoscope are made by light bouncing between the mirrors inside.

Equipment: Three small mirrors (all the same size), sticky tape, card or paper, coloured paper shapes or beads.

1. Tape the mirrors together in a triangle.
2. Stand them on the card or paper and draw round their shape.

3. Cut out the triangle of card or paper and tape it to one end of the mirrors.
4. Drop pieces of coloured paper or coloured beads inside.
5. Look inside your kaleidoscope. How many patterns can you see? Shake the kaleidoscope to change the pattern.

Mirror

Card or paper

Sticky tape

Pattern inside kaleidoscope

Make a Periscope

The commander of a submarine that is below the sea can find out what is happening above the surface by raising a special tube called a **periscope** up out of the water. A periscope uses two mirrors that bounce reflections between them so people can see round corners or look at things that are too high for them to see. You can make a periscope for yourself.

1. Draw three lines on the cardboard to divide it into four equal strips.
2. Cut squares in two of the strips as shown.
3. Cut two lines on each of the other two strips so they make an angle of 45° with the side of the card.
4. Fold the card into a tube shape and stick it together with tape.
5. Slide the mirrors into the angled slits and tape them in position. One mirror should face upwards and the other should face downwards.
6. If you hold the periscope sideways, you will be able to see round corners. If you hold it upright, you will be able to see over the heads of people or things that are taller than you are.

How it works
Light from the objects that are out of sight is reflected from the top mirror down into the lower mirror. You are able to see the objects by looking in the lower mirror.

Equipment: Two small, square mirrors, a piece of strong cardboard 30 cm × 30 cm (1 foot × 1 foot), sticky tape, ruler, protractor, scissors.

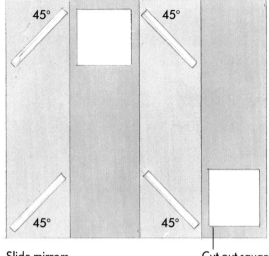

45°   45°

45°   45°

Slide mirrors into slits.

Cut out square of card.

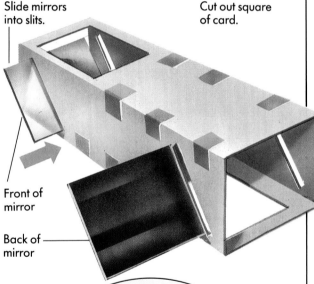

Front of mirror

Back of mirror

Light is reflected from one mirror to another.

Looking at Curved Mirrors

Curved mirrors produce images that are different from those you see in flat mirrors. Look at your face in the front and back of a shiny spoon. How are the images different?

Mirrors that curve outwards in the middle (like the back of a spoon) are called **convex** mirrors. They produce an image that is **smaller** than the one you would see in a flat mirror. Convex mirrors are attached to cars. They gather light from a wide area and give drivers a good view of what is happening behind them.

Mirrors that curve inwards in the middle (like the front of a spoon) are called **concave** mirrors. They give an image that is **larger** than the one you would see in a flat mirror. Convex mirrors are used for shaving and make-up mirrors. They are also used to make powerful telescopes (see pages 144–145).

▶ The strange mirrors that you see at some fairgrounds are partly convex and partly concave. Some parts of the reflections are stretched and other parts are squeezed up. People standing in front of mirrors like this look very funny!

Bending Light

Light travels at different speeds through different substances. It travels more slowly through water or glass than it does through air. As the light slows down, it also changes direction a little. This is called **refraction** and it makes the light rays look as if they 'bend' at the point where two substances meet.

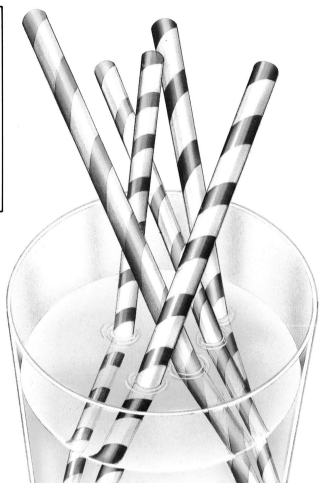

Water Can Bend Light

Fill a glass with water and place a straw in it. Look down at the straw as it stands in the water. You will see that the straw appears to bend. When you lift the straw out of the water you will see that it is still straight. The light rays change direction when they enter the water and make the straw look as if it bends in the middle. Look at your legs when they are half in and half out of the bathwater and you will see the same effect!

Magic Money

Equipment: A coin, a bowl or cup, water.

1. Put the bowl or cup on a table and place the coin in the bottom.
2. Keep looking at the coin and move slowly backwards until the coin disappears from view.
3. Stay standing in the same place and ask a friend to pour water into the cup or bowl. You will find you can see the coin again!

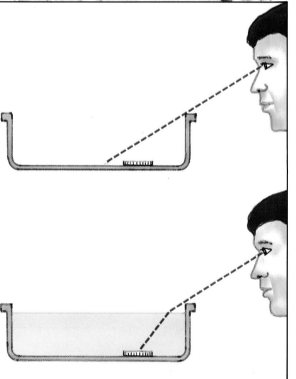

How it works
The light from the coin is 'bent' (refracted) by the water so you can see it again. Swimming pools and ponds never look as deep as they really are because light from the bottom is 'bent' before it reaches our eyes.

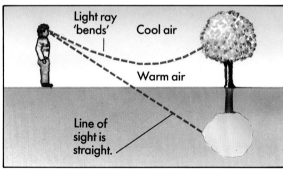

Air Can Bend Light

On a very hot day, you can sometimes see what looks like a pool of water on the road although the road is really completely dry! Light from the sky is 'bent' (refracted) by the hot air near the road and the 'pool' you see is actually refracted Sunlight. This is why people see 'mirages' in a desert (see photograph above). The hot air bends the light so objects that are really a long way away appear to be close by.

Glass Can Bend Light

Hold a pencil behind a thick glass dish so that half the pencil is above the dish and half is below. You will find that the part of the pencil behind the glass seems to be separated from the part of the pencil in the air. This is because light travels more slowly in glass than in air. The light rays change direction at the edge of the glass and make the pencil look as if it 'bends' in the middle.

Glass can be made into different shapes so that it 'bends' the light in different directions. Turn over to find out more about this.

141

Lenses

Transparent materials (such as water or glass), which can bend light rays by refraction, can work as lenses. Lenses are curved on one or both sides and are useful for bending light in special ways. They make objects look larger or smaller, depending on the shape of the lens. You can find out how lenses work on pages 144–145.

Lenses can be made of any clear material that has smooth, clear sides. You have a lens in each eye. People usually make lenses out of glass. They are used in spectacles, cameras, microscopes and telescopes. A microscope (right) uses several sets of lenses and can make tiny objects look hundreds or thousands of times bigger.

Making Things Look Larger...

Water sometimes acts as a lens and makes things look larger. Make a lens from a drop of water to see how this works.

Cut a small hole about 2.5 cm (1 inch) in diameter in a piece of card. Stick a piece of clear tape across the hole. Use a straw to carefully put a drop of water on the tape. Look at a leaf or a page from a newspaper through the drop of water and you will see that the object looks bigger through the lens.

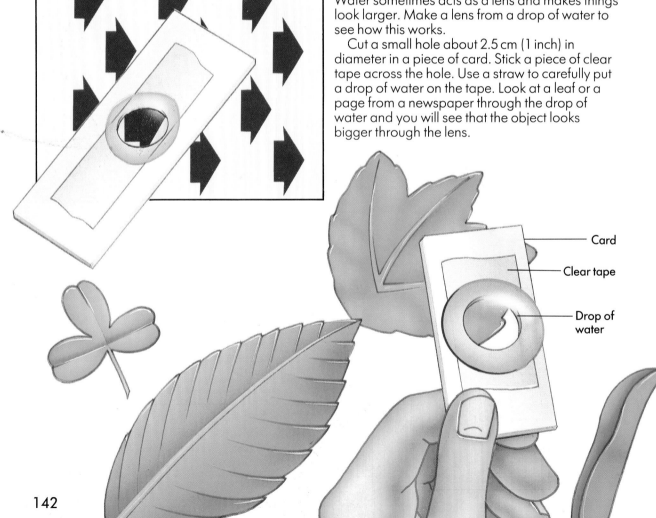

Card

Clear tape

Drop of water

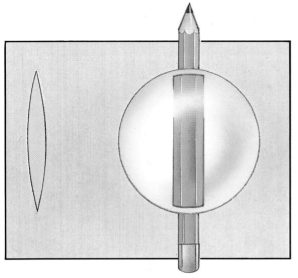

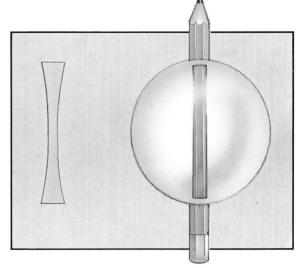

Convex lenses make things look bigger. They are thicker in the middle than they are at the edges so they curve outwards. This shape is called convex.

Concave lenses make things look smaller. They are thinner in the middle and thicker at the edges. This shape is called concave.

... and Smaller

Ask if you can borrow the spectacles of a person who is short-sighted. (He or she finds it difficult to see things that are a long way off.) Try holding the spectacles a little way above the print of this page and look through the lens. You will notice that the print looks very tiny.

If you cannot borrow spectacles ... try looking through the bottom of a very thick glass. (This will not work quite as well as the spectacles. The letters may be bent out of shape because the glass is not curved exactly.)

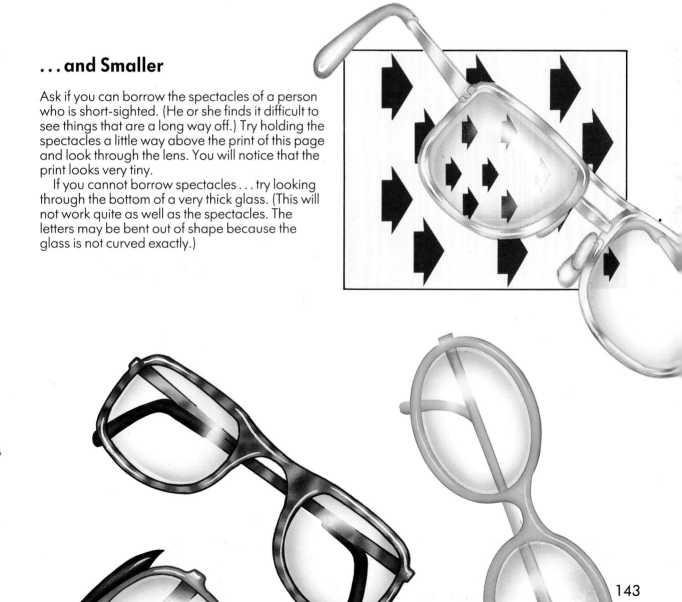

143

How Lenses Work

1. Cut a hole in the card about 2.5 cm (1 inch) in diameter and tape the comb over the hole.
2. In a darkened room, stand the card in front of a beam of light from a torch.
3. Lay the white paper in front of the rays of light that come through the comb so you can see them clearly. (You may need to place the paper on top of some books.)
4. Hold the magnifying glass against the edge of the paper and notice what happens to the rays of light.

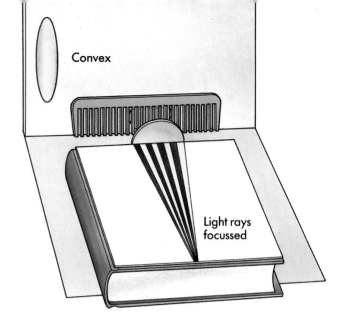

Convex

Light rays focussed

Telescopes

One lens held close to a small object can make it look larger but to look at things that are a long way off you need a telescope. Telescopes make things look closer so they can be seen more clearly and studied in detail.

▶ Amateur astronomers use telescopes like this to observe the night sky. This type of telescope reveals details on the surface of the Moon and makes it possible to see the rings around Saturn. It can even be used to study galaxies about 50 million light years away.

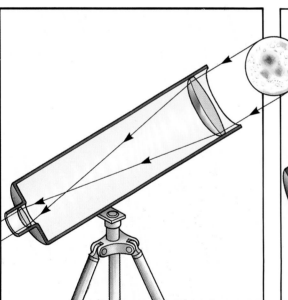

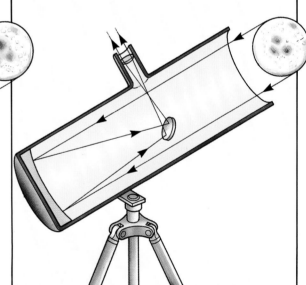

Some telescopes are called **refracting** telescopes because they have two lenses that refract (bend) the light. A large lens collects and focusses the light and a smaller lens makes the image larger so it can be seen clearly.

Other telescopes are called **reflecting** telescopes because they use mirrors to reflect the light. A large, curved mirror reflects the light onto a smaller, flatter mirror which in turn reflects the image onto a small lens. The lens makes the image look larger.

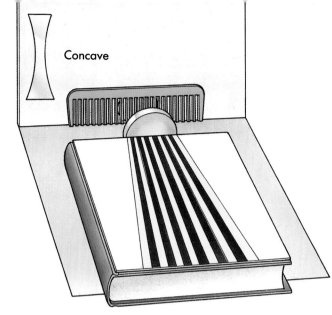

Concave

Equipment: A sheet of card, a comb, a torch, sticky tape, a magnifying glass, a sheet of white paper, books (optional).

How it works
The magnifying glass is a convex lens. It bends the rays so they all come together at a point. This is called **focussing** the light.

Now repeat the investigation using a concave lens, such as the spectacles of a short-sighted person. In this sort of lens the middle of the lens curves inwards. This time you will see that the beams of light are spread out instead of being focussed.

Make a Telescope

Equipment: A shaving mirror, a small, flat mirror, a magnifying glass.

1. Stand the shaving mirror by a window pointing towards the Stars or the Moon.
2. Hold the flat mirror so you can see a reflection of the shaving mirror in the middle.
3. Look at the reflection in the flat mirror using the magnifying glass. The stars or Moon will look much nearer through the glass lens.

The first reflecting telescope like this was made by Isaac Newton in the mid-17th century.

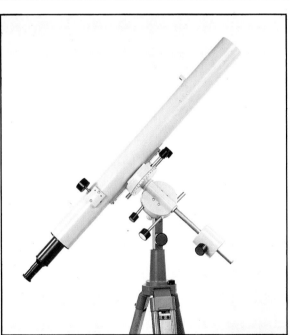

Warning: Never look directly at the Sun (especially through lenses or telescopes). You will damage your eyes.

Light and Sight

When your eyes are open, the light reflected from objects around you enters your eyes through the **pupil** – the black hole in the middle. The pupil is an opening in the coloured part of the eye, which is called the **iris**. A **lens** behind the **iris** focusses the light onto a light-sensitive layer called the **retina** at the back of the eye. Special optical nerves carry messages from the retina to the brain, which interprets the images so you can see.

Pupil Power

The pupil in the middle of the eye can change size to control the amount of light entering the eye. You can see this happening if you look closely into your own eyes. Stay in a dimly lit room for several minutes. Look into the mirror and notice the size of your pupils. Then turn on a bright light or move into a brightly lit place and look again at your pupils.

Dark   Light

In dim light, the pupils open wide to let in as much light as possible. In bright light, they become very small to stop too much light from reaching the retina and damaging this sensitive layer.

◄ Cut-away view inside a human eye. The image of the person is upside down because the rays of light travel in straight lines and cross over behind the lens.

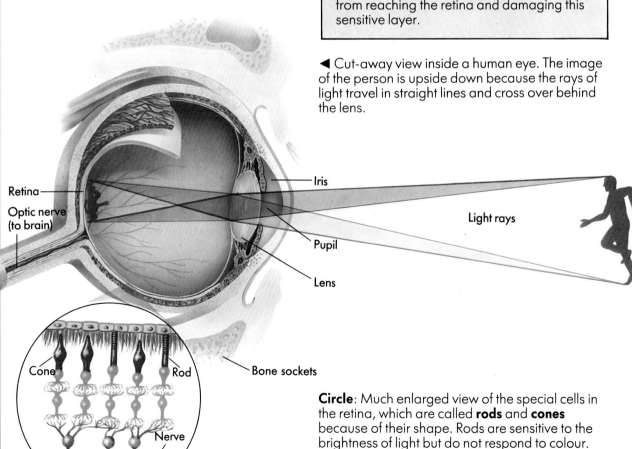

Retina

Optic nerve (to brain)

Iris

Light rays

Pupil

Lens

Cone   Rod

Nerve

Bone sockets

Circle: Much enlarged view of the special cells in the retina, which are called **rods** and **cones** because of their shape. Rods are sensitive to the brightness of light but do not respond to colour. Rods work well when the light is dim. The cones are sensitive to bright light and to colour. They allow you to see things in colour.

Make a Model Eye

Equipment: A round bowl with water inside, black card, white card, a small table lamp without a shade.

1. Make a small hole in the middle of the black card – this represents the pupil in your eye.
2. Place the black card on one side of the bowl and the white card (which represents the retina) on the other side.
3. Place the lamp so it is in line with the two cards and switch on the lamp.
4. Turn off any other lights in the room and pull the curtains (if necessary) to make the room dim.

5. Move the white card to and fro until an image of the lamp appears on it.

How it works

The image you see will be small and upside down. The image that forms on the retina in the back of your eyes is also upside down but your brain is used to this and can interpret the images so you see things the right way up.

Black card

White card

Image is upside down.

Short-Sight and Long-Sight

Some people cannot focus on things a long way off. This is because the lens in one or both of their eyes focusses the image in **front** of the retina so the image that forms on the retina is blurred. This is called being **short-sighted** and can be corrected by wearing spectacles with concave lenses.

The Disappearing Rabbit

At the back of the eye is a large nerve (the optic nerve) which leads to the brain. At this part of the retina there are no rods or cones so if light is focussed here you cannot see anything. You will see this effect if you try this trick.

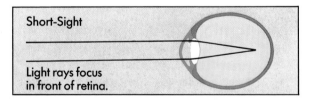

Short-Sight

Light rays focus in front of retina.

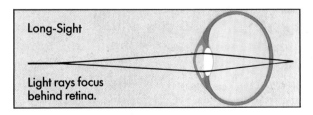

Long-Sight

Light rays focus behind retina.

Other people cannot focus on things close to them because the lens forms a clear image **behind** the retina. This is called being **long-sighted** and can be corrected with convex lenses.

Hold the book up in front of your face at a normal reading distance. Shut your left eye and stare at the magician's wand. Slowly move the book closer to your eye and the rabbit will disappear!

Using Two Eyes

Because you have two eyes you see two images of everything you look at. Each eye looks at the world around you from a slightly different position. This allows you to see things in three dimensions rather than just as a flat picture. It also helps you to judge distances and appreciate perspective.

How Many Pencils?

1. Place a glass of water on a table and stand a pencil about 30 cm (1 foot) behind it.
2. Look through the jar and you will see the images of two pencils in it.
3. Close your left eye and the right hand pencil will disappear. Close your right eye and the left hand pencil will disappear.

How it works
The water is working as a lens to produce the images but because the water is held in a cylinder shape each eye looks through the water at a slightly different angle. So, with both eyes open, you see two pencils. With one eye open you see only one image.

Fly the Rocket to the Moon

Hold the book so your nose touches the dot in the middle of the picture below. Turn the book round slowly in an anti-clockwise direction. You should see the rocket fly into space and land on the Moon!

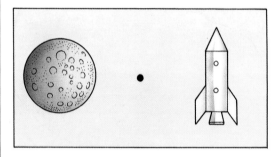

How it works
Each eye sends a slightly different message to the brain. The right eye sees the rocket and the left eye sees the Moon. Your brain combines the two pictures and makes the rocket appear to fly.

Touch the Dot

Draw a dot on a piece of paper and put the paper about 75 cm (2½ feet) in front of you on a table. Sit at the table, put a hand in front of one eye and use your other hand to try and touch the dot with a pencil.

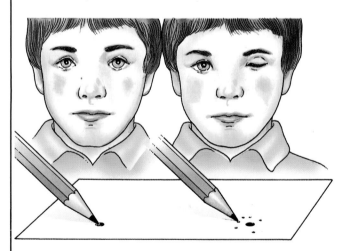

You will find it quite difficult to touch the dot accurately at the first attempt because you cannot judge distances easily with only one eye. You use both eyes to find the exact position of things.

Hole in the Hand

Find a cardboard tube or roll up a piece of paper to make a long tube. Look through the tube with your right eye and hold your left hand up next to the paper with the palm towards you. You should see that there seems to be a hole through the middle of your palm!

How it works
Your right eye sees inside the tube and your left eye sees your open hand. The brain is confused because it receives such different signals from each eye. So it combines the images and you appear to see a hole in your hand.

Make a 3-D Viewer

Equipment: Card, pencil, ruler, scissors.

1. Trace this cross shape onto the card using the pencil and ruler. Make the cross 5 cm (2 inches) high and make each arm of the cross about 1.3 cm (½ inch) wide.
2. Cut out the cross shape to leave a hole in the card.
3. Hold the card upright at right angles to a picture or photograph.
4. Stare hard down through the cross for a few seconds and you should see the picture stand out in three dimensions. (It helps if you **expect** this to happen.)

How it works
The cross shape hides the edges of the picture so you cannot see that it is really flat. Your brain is used to seeing the world in three dimensions and makes the picture **appear** to be three dimensional.

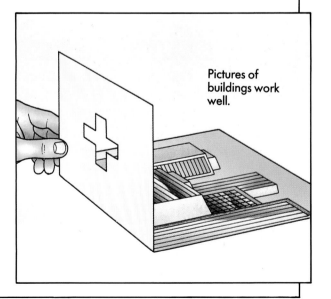

Pictures of buildings work well.

Fool Your Eyes

Here are some tricks to fool your eyes so that objects appear to move when they are really still and you see objects that are not really there at all! You can also find out how a confusing background changes the shape or size of an object.

See the Ghost in the Castle

Hold this book up in front of you about 30 cm (1 foot) from your eyes. Stare hard at the black ghost and concentrate on its face. Count slowly to thirty. Then immediately look into the archway of the castle. Count to ten and you will see a white ghost appear!

How it works
When you stared at the black ghost, the part of the retina on which the image was formed did not receive any bright light. But the surrounding area worked hard to send back messages to your brain about the bright, white background around the ghost. When you looked at the archway, the area that had formed an image of the

Turn on the Music

Look at this picture of a record on a turntable and move the book slowly round in a circle. Your eyes cannot follow the dark and light stripes round and round because they keep changing their position so quickly. Your brain interprets the picture as a record turning, which is what it **expects** to see.

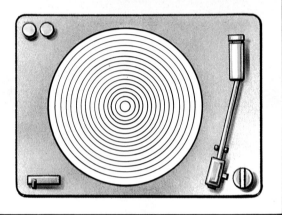

background was tired and did not respond fully to the white of the archway. This made some of the archway appear slightly grey. But the area of the retina that formed the image of the ghost did work properly and made some of the archway (in the shape of the ghost) appear white. This is why you see a white, ghostly image in the archway.

Confusing Backgrounds

Are all these figures the same size?

Look at these diagrams carefully. The three figures are all the same size but the background lines make the figure on the right appear to be larger than the others. The background pattern in the diagram below confuses the eyes and brain and makes the circle look as if it is not a true circle.

Is this circle round?

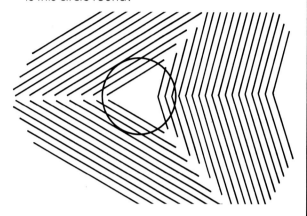

Clues to Size and Distance

Our eyes use many clues from our surroundings to work out how far away things are and how big they are. We often compare the size of things with other objects close by. This gives us a sense of perspective. Look at these examples of pictures that have confusing clues and make it difficult to judge distance and perspective properly.

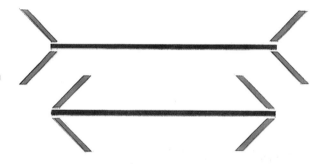

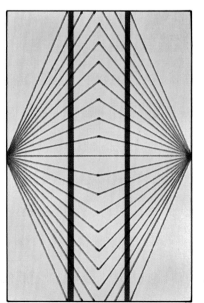

In the diagrams above, the two horizontal lines are the same length but the angle of the arrows makes one line look longer than the other.

In these two diagrams, the two vertical lines appear to be bent but they are really straight.

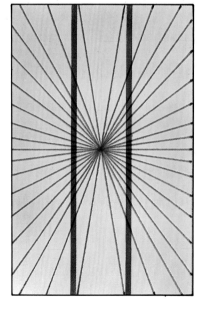

Moving Pictures

If your eyes see two pictures very quickly, one after the other, they may not be able to tell that the picture has changed and the image will appear to move. You can only register 12 pictures a second as separate images. If the pictures appear more quickly than this, you see them as moving pictures. Films that you see at the cinema have 24 photographs (frames) every second.

How to Make Pictures Move

Before films were invented, people produced moving pictures using a set of drawings. Each one was slightly different from the one before. The drawings were made into a book, which was flicked quickly with a thumb. This made the pictures appear quickly one after the other so the eyes saw a steady movement. You can try this for yourself, first with just two pictures then with a whole series.

Put the Fish in the Bowl

1. Draw a fish and a bowl separately on a piece of card. Put the fish on one side of the card and the bowl on the other.
2. Fix the card to a thin rod or pencil with tape.
3. Hold the rod or pencil between the palms of your hands.
4. Rub your hands together to twist the rod or pencil quickly backwards and forwards. You should see the fish appear in the bowl!

The Happy and Sad Face

1. On a card or piece of white paper, draw the outline of a face with a big grin.
2. Lay a piece of tracing paper over the face and stick it with tape on the left hand side.
3. Trace the face onto the tracing paper but this time give the face a frown instead of a grin.
4. Roll the tracing paper carefully around a pencil.
5. Move the pencil rapidly from left to right, rolling and unrolling the tracing paper as you do so. Watch the expression on the face change from happy to sad. Can you think of other pictures to try this with?

Make Your Own Movie

Equipment: Paper, pencil, needle and thread (or a small notebook).

Find a notebook with small pages or make your own tiny book. To do this, cut the paper into 10 (or more) squares about 7.5 cm × 7.5 cm (3 inches × 3 inches). Fold the pieces of paper in half and stitch the book together along the fold using a needle and thread. (Ask an adult to help you do this if the paper is rather thick.)

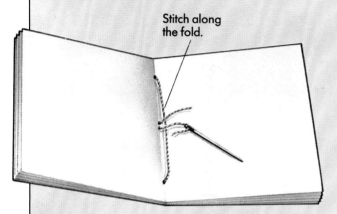

Stitch along the fold.

On each page of the book draw one of the pictures in the sequence to the right. You could make up your own pictures instead so long as each image is only slightly different from the one before. Make sure you draw on only one side of the page. When the book is complete, flick the pages with your thumb and see the story come to life.

Rainbow Colours

Sunlight or the light from an electric light bulb appears colourless and is called 'white light'. But it is really made up of a mixture of different colours. We can only see these colours when light passes through a transparent substance (such as water or glass), which separates the colours into a rainbow pattern called a **spectrum**. A spectrum consists of seven colours – red, orange, yellow, green, blue, indigo and violet – as well as two other kinds of light (ultra-violet and infra-red), which we cannot see. You can see a spectrum in bubbles of water or in a rainbow.

Make a Rainbow

A 17th century scientist called Isaac Newton was the first person to show that light can be split up into different colours. He used a small piece of glass with triangular sides (called a **prism**) to do this. You can use a bowl of water and a mirror instead of a prism.

On a sunny day, fill a bowl with water and rest a flat mirror against the inside. Stand the bowl so that Sunlight falls onto the mirror. Hold a sheet of white card in front of the mirror and move it around until a rainbow of colours appears on it. You may have to adjust the position of the mirror to get this just right. Once the mirror and card are in the correct position, you can keep the mirror still with a little modelling clay.

How it works
The 'wedge' of water between the mirror and the surface of the water acts as a prism and splits up the light so you can see the different colours. This happens because each of the colours in white light travels at a slightly different speed and is bent (refracted – see pages 140–141) inside the prism by a different amount. Violet light bends the most and red light bends the least.

More things to try
Put a magnifying glass between the mirror and the card. You should find that the lens bends the light so the colours come back together again and the rainbow disappears! This shows that the seven colours of the rainbow combine to make white light.

Colour Spinners

Here is another way to show that white light is made up of the seven colours of the rainbow.

51°

Equipment: Card, scissors, a short pencil with a sharp point or a pointed stick.

1. Cut out a disc with a diameter of 10 cm (4 inches).
2. Divide it into seven equal sections. Make each section about 51° wide. Use a protractor to divide up the disc.
3. Colour each section with one of the colours of the spectrum.
4. Make a small hole in the middle of the disc and push the sharp pencil or stick through.
5. Spin the disc quickly. What do you see?

More things to try

● Make another disc in the same way but divide it into three sections. Colour one section red, one blue and one green. When you spin the disc it will look greyish white again. This is because red, blue and green are the main colours our eyes are able to respond to. They are called the **primary colours** of light.
● Try different combinations of two of the primary colours. Make a spinner that is half red and half green and one that is half red and half blue. What colours do you see when you spin the discs? (You will find this is different from mixing coloured paints.)

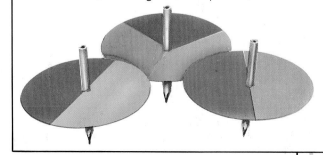

How it works

When the circle spins quickly, your eyes cannot see each colour separately. You see only the result of mixing the different coloured light together. This is why the disc appears greyish white even though there are really seven colours on it.

What Colour is it?

Most objects do not produce light of their own. They reflect the light that falls on them and our eyes see the reflected light. So the colour of an object depends on the colour of light that it reflects back into our eyes.

▶ The colours you see depend on the sort of light that falls on objects. Yellow sodium street lights make some colours look very bright. These colours are used in safety equipment and clothing, to make them show up clearly at night.

Explaining Colours

White objects reflect all the colours of light.

Coloured objects reflect certain colours and absorb the rest. We see the reflected colour. A red shirt looks red because it reflects more of the red part of the spectrum than any other colour. It absorbs most of the other colours in the light that shines on it.

Black objects reflect hardly any of the light that falls on them. But even black things reflect some light. The only thing that can be completely black is a hole. Try an experiment to prove this.

Find a box with a lid and cut a small hole in one end of the box. Paint the inside of the box and the surface around the hole black. When you look at the painted surface, it will look black but the hole will seem to be much darker. Any light that goes into the box through the hole bounces from one side of the box to the other. The hole does not reflect any light so it is completely dark.

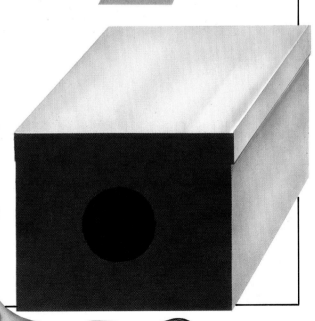

No Way Through

Most materials reflect all the light that shines on them and do not let any light pass through. They are called **opaque** materials. Some examples are: paper, metal, stone and cloth.

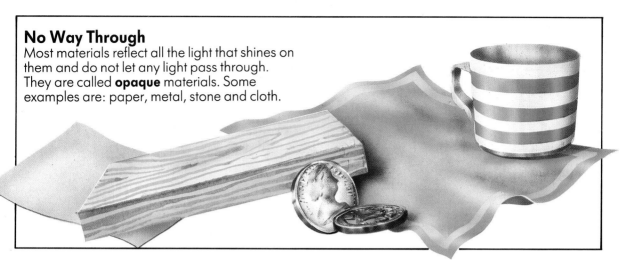

See-Through Objects

Some materials reflect hardly any light at all. The light passes right through so you can see through them. They are called **transparent** materials. Glass and water are transparent; how many objects made of transparent materials can you think of? (You can find out more about transparent materials on pages 158–159.)

Some Light Gets Through

A few materials reflect some light but also let some light pass through. These are called **translucent** materials. Some examples are: frosted glass, thick plastic and tracing paper. If you look through a translucent material, things will look blurred.

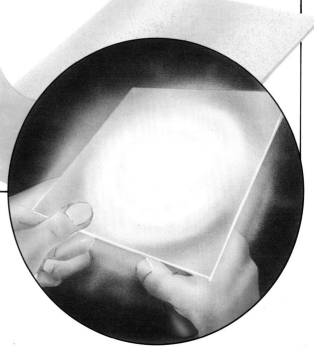

This is because the light is bent in all directions.

Spot the Difference

You can check to see if an object is translucent or transparent by shining a torch behind it in a darkened room. If you can see the light clearly, the object is transparent. If the object looks blurred, the object is translucent.

Changing Colour

Transparent materials can be used to make colour filters, which change the colour of the objects that you see through them. A colour filter only allows light of its own colour to pass through.

Make a Viewing Box

Try this experiment to see what happens to the colour of objects when you view them in different coloured light.

Equipment: A cardboard box with a lid, coloured cellophane, tape, coloured objects, scissors.

1. First make colour filters. Cut frames from the card about 10 cm × 7 cm (4 inches × 3 inches) in size. Stick a piece of cellophane onto each one.
2. Cut a rectangle out of the lid of the box. (Make it slightly smaller than the frames.)
3. Cut a viewing hole in the side of the box.
4. Place a red cellophane filter over the lid.
5. Put one red object (such as a tomato) and one green object (such as an apple) inside the box. Shine a torch through the filter. What colour do the objects appear to be when you look through the viewing hole?

How it works
The red filter allows only red light to pass through into the box. The red tomato looks pale because it reflects mainly red light, which can pass through the filter. The green apple reflects mainly green

Turn the World Red

Set up a water prism to make a spectrum on a piece of card (see page 154) or colour your own rainbow on a piece of white paper. Look at your rainbow through a piece of red cellophane. What happens to the spectrum?

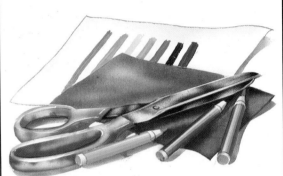

How it works
You will find that only red light appears on the card. The cellophane is transparent so it lets light pass through it. But it is also red, which means that it absorbs all the colours of the spectrum except red. So only red light shines through on to the card. (The cellophane also reflects some red light so it appears red when you look at it.)

light, which is stopped by the filter. The apple appears dark because there is no light reflected from it. Try looking at the same two objects through a green filter. Does the apple or the tomato look dark this time? Experiment with different coloured filters and other objects as well.

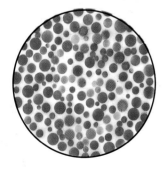

Some people cannot see the difference between red and green. They will not be able to see the letter 'S' in the diagram above. This is one form of colour blindness.

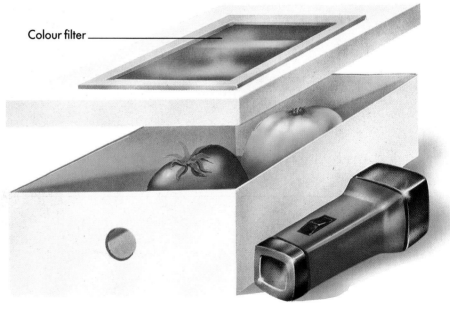

Colour filter

▲ Colour filters are used to produce spectacular light effects at discotheques.

Make a Stained Glass Window

Stained glass windows also act as colour filters. You can make your own with some thin card and coloured cellophane or tissue paper.

1. Choose a pattern to put on your window. It can be anything from a rocket to a bumble bee. Draw your design on the card.
2. Decide on your colour scheme and mark the different coloured areas on the card.
3. Cut out the shapes from the card but remember to leave enough card between the different areas so you can stick the coloured cellophane or tissue down.
4. Cut the coloured cellophane or tissue to fit behind the holes. Allow a little extra on each piece to stick to the card.
5. Fix the coloured shapes on to the card with glue or sticky tape and hang your stained glass window in the light.

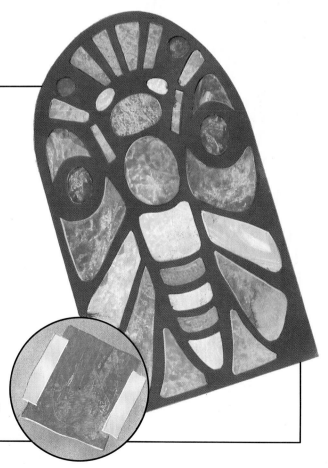

Separating Colours

Coloured objects are able to reflect some of the colours in the light that falls on them because they contain substances called **pigments**. You can find out more about pigments by investigating the inks and dyes that people use to colour things.

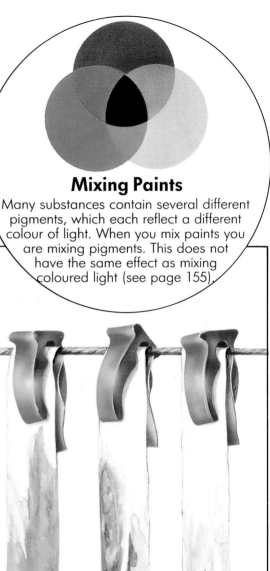

Mixing Paints

Many substances contain several different pigments, which each reflect a different colour of light. When you mix paints you are mixing pigments. This does not have the same effect as mixing coloured light (see page 155).

Investigating Inks and Dyes

Here is a way for you to separate the different coloured pigments in some inks and dyes.
Equipment: White blotting paper (or large coffee filters), a dish or saucer of water, inks or dyes (such as food colouring, felt pens).

1. Cut the blotting paper or filter paper into long strips about 2 cm × 30 cm (1 inch × 1 foot).
2. Put a drop of the ink or dye you want to test about 4 cm (1½ inches) from one end of the paper.
3. Hang the paper strip up so that the end with the drop of ink or dye on it just dips into the saucer of water. You will soon see coloured bands spreading up the paper.
4. Take each strip of paper out of the water when the colour is nearly at the top. Let the paper dry and you will be able to examine the colours closely.

How it works
The paper soaks up water from the saucer and the water carries the different colours up the paper. The different coloured pigments travel at different speeds up the paper so you will be able to see separate bands of colour. This is called **chromatography**. Some inks and dyes contain only one colour but others are mixtures of two or more colours.

Tie Dyeing

Tie dyeing works by preventing dye reaching some parts of the cloth so that white patterns are left in the coloured material.

Equipment: An old handkerchief (or old piece of cloth), string or thread, a cold water dye from a hardware store (or make your own dyes.)

1. Make up the dye according to the instructions.
2. Decide where you would like the patterns to appear on the cloth. Pull a cone of fabric from these areas through your finger or thumb and tie a piece of thread tightly around it. Then tie a second piece of thread or string just below the first one.
3. Complete the dyeing process and then cut the threads.

How it works
The tight threads keep the dye away from the material just below them. These areas stay white and make flower-shaped patterns.

Make Your Own Dyes

Long before artificial dyes were invented, people used natural dyes from plants and the soil to colour their clothes, pottery and other objects in their homes. You can try making some dyes for yourself.

Try out the dyes on pieces of white cloth, such as an old handkerchief or squares cut from an old sheet. (Do not use your best shirt as some of the dyes are permanent!) Make sure the cloth is clean and dry. Do not use cloth that has been treated with fabric softeners. These chemicals may stop the dye working.

Method for Plant Dyes
Boil the leaves or fruit with a little water in a saucepan. Simmer for about 15 minutes and allow to cool. An alternative method is to put the plant material in a bowl and cover it with boiling water. Leave the bowl to stand for about 15 minutes.

Then make a filter. Cut the top half off a plastic bottle, turn it upside down and put a coffee filter inside. Pour the liquid from the saucepan or bowl through the filter to produce a coloured liquid that you can use for dyeing.

Warning: Ask an adult to help you with these experiments as boiling water is dangerous and you might burn yourself. Wear an apron or overall to protect your clothes.

Colours to Try
● **Red** – Beetroot, cherries, red cabbage
● **Yellow** – Onion skins
● **Green** – Spinach
● **Brown** – Iodine, tea, coffee (about 2 teaspoonfuls in half a cup of water).
● **Blue** – Dissolve a spoonful of flour in half a cup of warm water and add one or two drops of iodine.

Light for Life

Green plants need light from the Sun to make their food. Without Sunlight, green plants will die. Without green plants, all life on Earth would be unable to survive. All living things feed on plants or animals that have eaten plants.

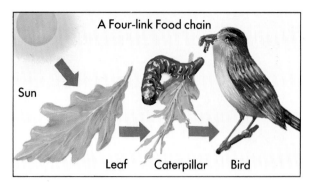

A Four-link Food chain

Sun — Leaf — Caterpillar — Bird

▲ The Sun's light energy is trapped by green plants, which are in turn eaten by animals. Food chains link together to form food webs because most animals have several kinds of food.

Plants and Light

Try this experiment to prove that green plants need light to survive.

Find a sheet of cardboard and lay it across a patch of grass. Leave it in place for several days, then lift it up and examine the grass underneath. You will see that the grass looks yellow and unhealthy. If you remove the cardboard after you have finished your experiment, the grass will slowly recover.

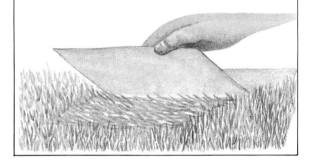

Bow to the Light

Plants grow towards the light so they get as much light as possible. If light is all around them, they grow straight up. If the light comes from one side only, they will grow towards the source of light and bend over. Try growing seeds to see this happen.

Sow some mustard and cress seeds in a little soil on two old saucers. Find a small box with a lid and cut a small hole in one side. Place one saucer in the box and put the lid on. Leave the other saucer in the open. Allow the seeds to grow for about a week. Do they grow differently?

Remember to water the soil if it becomes dry.

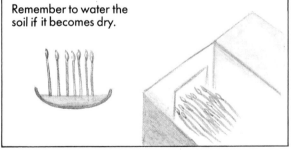

Grass grows taller inside 'greenhouse'.

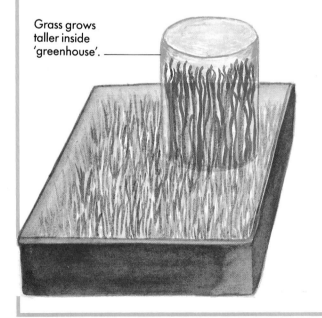

Greenhouses

A greenhouse provides a warm atmosphere for growing plants. Light and heat from the Sun passes through the glass and heats up the air inside. This heat cannot escape easily and the air inside stays warmer than the air outside. You can see the effect of a greenhouse by placing a glass jar over a patch of grass or over one section of the seeds growing in a seed tray. Inside your 'greenhouse' the plants will grow faster.

Cats' eyes seem to glow in the dark. This is because they have an extra reflective layer at the back of their eyes, behind the retina. At night, when only a small amount of light enters a cat's eyes, the light is reflected back through the retina again. This helps to produce a clear image. Many mammals have this special layer in their eyes; it is called a **tapetum**.

Some animals can produce light. Firefly beetles attract a mate with flashes of light. Different kinds of firefly signal with different patterns of flashes, which helps each individual to recognize others of its own kind.

Some animals use light and colour to help them hide from their enemies. This is called **camouflage**. The bush cricket above looks just like a leaf, for example. The stripes on a tiger's body help to break up its outline and make it difficult to see among tall grasses. This helps it to creep up on the animals it hunts without being seen.

Looking at Sunlight

Sunlight contains two types of rays that we cannot see. They are called ultra-violet and infra-red rays. The **ultra-violet** rays cause our skin to turn a darker colour. The skin darkens to prevent the ultra-violet rays from getting through and damaging the body. Suntan creams contain substances that cut down the amount of ultra-violet light that reaches the skin. The heat of the sun comes from **infra-red** rays. These rays can burn the skin if they are too strong.

Heat from the Sun

The heat from the Sun warms everything on Earth. The land heats up more quickly than the sea but it also cools down more quickly too. You may have noticed that the sea is warmer than the land if you have walked barefoot along a beach in the evening.

1. Fill one of the containers with water and the other with dry soil or potting compost.

2. Place a thermometer in each container and stand them in a sunny place. Note down the temperature in each container.

Equipment: Two containers, two thermometers, dry soil, water, black cloth.

3. Cover the containers with a black cloth and leave them in the Sun for about two hours. Note down the temperature every half hour. Which container heats up more quickly? Which one reaches the highest temperature?

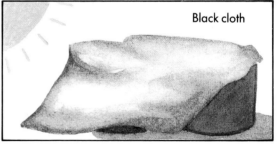

4. Now put the two containers in a cool place out of the Sun. Which container cools down more quickly?

Bake a Potato

You can use the infra-red rays from the Sun to cook food and prepare a feast for yourself. Microwave ovens cook food in a similar way.

1. Line the basket with the foil; put the shiny side outwards. Make the foil as smooth as possible and tape it in position. (It helps to put a liner under the foil.)
2. Push the nail or fork through the middle of the base of the basket and fix the small potato to it.
3. Set up your 'cooker' facing the Sun. To get the best results, you should do this on a **very** hot day around noon.
4. Turn the 'cooker' to face the Sun as it moves across the sky.

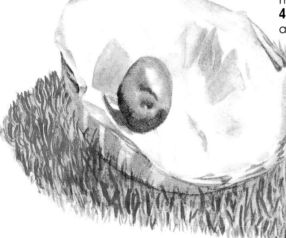

How it works
The tin foil reflects the Sun's rays like a mirror and concentrates them on the potato. The heat warms the potato and should eventually cook it through to the middle if the Sun is hot enough.

Equipment: A small potato, tin foil, a round hanging basket frame (and liner if possible) or a round metal bowl, a long nail or fork, sticky tape.

Using Light from the Sun

Solar panels are used in the roofs or sides of buildings to collect heat from the Sun. The heat is used to warm rooms and provide hot water. Solar panels are arranged to face the Sun for as much of the day as possible. Some kinds can be turned to follow the Sun as it moves across the sky. In sunny places, solar panels can be used to provide most of the energy for a home. In other places, they can be used as well as other sources of energy, such as electricity. They are also used on satellites.

Laser Light

Machines called lasers strengthen light energy to produce a narrow beam of light that is amazingly powerful. A laser beam can cut a hole through a steel plate in seconds and can produce a disc of light on the Moon. Low-powered lasers are used by doctors to carry out delicate operations. Laser beams also carry signals in video disc players.

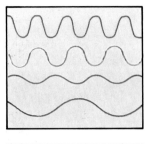

Ordinary (white) light is a mixture of wavelengths (colours) and the waves overlap.

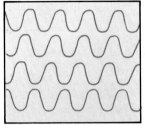

Light of one colour is all one wavelength and the waves overlap.

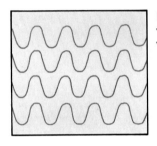

Laser light is all one wavelength and the waves are all in step.

A Special Light

Ordinary light from the Sun or an electric light bulb is a mixture of different colours. Each colour is produced by light of a different wavelength and the waves overlap each other. But in a beam of laser light, the light is only one colour so it is all the same wavelength. The waves are also all in step with each other. A laser sends out a narrow beam of light in only one direction and has a lot of energy because it concentrates the light.

How Lasers Work

Inside a laser is a crystal (such as a ruby) or a tube of gas, (such as carbon dioxide, krypton or argon). A source of energy (for example a flashing light) directs energy into the crystal or gas. When enough energy has built up, it is released as an intense beam of laser light. The diagram below shows a laser with a ruby crystal inside.

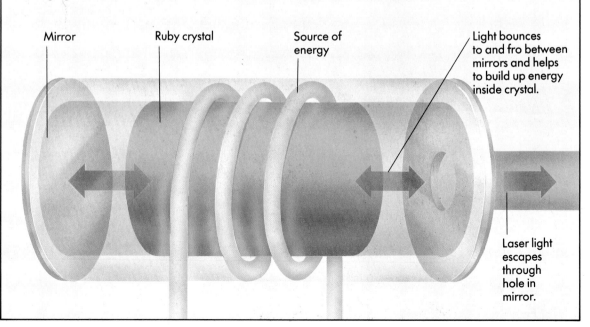

Mirror

Ruby crystal

Source of energy

Light bounces to and fro between mirrors and helps to build up energy inside crystal.

Laser light escapes through hole in mirror.

▲ Laser beams do not spread out like ordinary light beams so they can be used for accurate drilling operations. This laser is being used to drill a hole in aluminium.

◄ Lasers can be used to produce three dimensional pictures called holograms.

Light Quiz

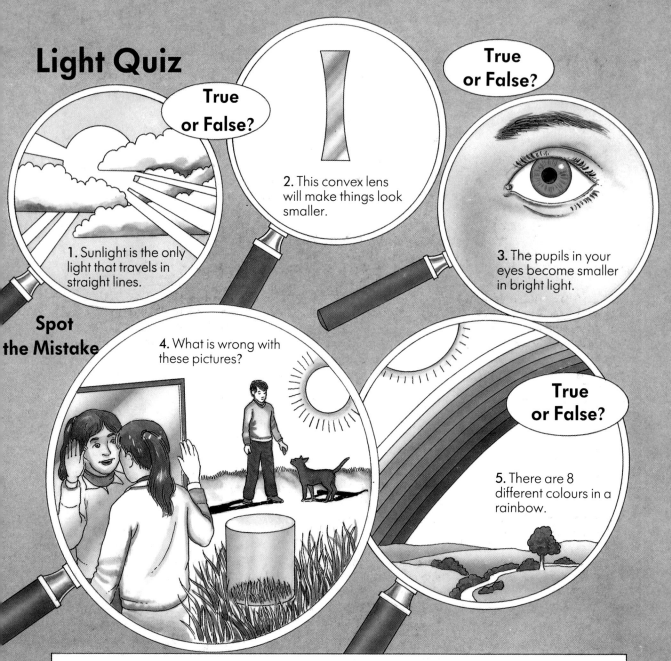

True or False?

1. Sunlight is the only light that travels in straight lines.

2. This convex lens will make things look smaller.

True or False?

3. The pupils in your eyes become smaller in bright light.

Spot the Mistake

4. What is wrong with these pictures?

True or False?

5. There are 8 different colours in a rainbow.

Answers

1. *False. All light travels in straight lines (page 166).*

2. *False. Convex lenses are enlarging or magnifying lenses (pages 143).*

3. *True. The pupils become smaller to prevent too much light entering the eyes and damaging the light sensitive layer (the retina) at the back of the eyes (page 146).*

4. *Left: Mirrors reverse images so the reflection in the mirror should show the other hand raised (page 136).*
Middle: The jar acts like a greenhouse so the grass under the jar would grow taller than the grass around it (page 162).
Right: All the shadows should be facing in the same direction (pages 132-133).

5. *False. There are only seven colours in a rainbow — red, orange, yellow, green, blue, indigo and violet (page 154).*

Glossary

Atmosphere A layer of gases that surrounds the Earth and consists mainly of nitrogen and oxygen.

Capillary attraction The effect of surface tension pulling the surface of a liquid up into narrow tubes.

Centrifugal force The force that pulls an object moving in a circle away from the centre of the circle so it tends to fly outwards.

Concave Curved inwards. A concave lens is thinner at the centre than the edges. It makes light rays spread apart so objects appear to be smaller.

Centre of gravity The point at which an object balances perfectly.

Condensation Tiny drops of liquid formed when a gas or vapour changes into a liquid.

Contract To make or become smaller (or shorten). Many metals contract as they cool down; so does air.

Convection The transfer of heat through a liquid or gas by the movement of the material itself. Convection takes place because gases or liquids expand when they are heated, become less dense (heavy) and rise above cooler gases or liquids that surround them.

Convex Curved outwards. A convex lens is thicker at the centre than the edges. It makes light rays come together so objects appear larger.

Density The amount of weight a substance has for its size. The density of a substance is worked out by dividing its weight in gm by its volume in cm^3.

Evaporation The change from a solid or liquid into a vapour; (the opposite of condensation).

Expand To swell out or increase in size, often as a result of being heated.

Filter To separate solids or suspended particles from a liquid by passing it through a layer of sand, fibre or charcoal.

Focus To bring rays of light together after they have been reflected or bent so they come to a point (also called a focus) and form a clear image.

Friction A force that tends to stop movement between any two surfaces that are moving over each other.

Gears Combination of wheels with teeth (cogs) around the edge that work on one another to change the speed of movement or direction.

Gravity The pulling force that draws objects towards the centre of the Earth. Gravity keeps everything on Earth from flying off into space and causes objects to have a weight.

Holography A technique by which laser light is used to photograph objects and reproduce them in three dimensions.

Inertia The tendency of something to stay still or keep moving.

Infra-red ('Below the red') light Rays with a wavelength just longer than the light at the red end of the part of the spectrum we can see. Infra-red light is invisible to our eyes but we feel it as heat.

Insulation A layer of material around an object that will not allow heat (or electricity or sound) to pass through it.

Laser A special device used to produce a very powerful, concentrated beam of light with all the waves in step with one another. The word 'laser' stands for **L**ight **A**mplification by **S**timulated **E**mission of **R**adiation.

Lens A transparent substance (usually glass) that has one or more curved sufaces. Lenses can bend the rays of light that pass through them to make things appear larger or smaller.

Opaque Not allowing rays of light to pass through. We cannot see through opaque substances.

Pendulum An object that is suspended so it can swing freely. The object may be connected to a piece of string or a rod.

Pulley A device consisting of wheels with grooves around the edges for ropes to fit into. Pulleys are used to increase the lifting power of a pulling force so that heavy objects can be lifted more easily.

Refraction The change in the direction of light rays at the surface between two substances, such as air and water. It occurs because light travels at different speeds in different substances.

Siphon A pipe or tube that is used to draw liquid from one place to another. As long as the tube remains full of liquid, and one end is held lower than the container in which the other end has been placed, then air pressure forces liquid up the lower end, over the bend in the tube and down the other side.

Spectrum of white light Band of seven different colours – red, orange, yellow, green, blue, indigo and violet. Each colour corresponds to a different wavelength.

Surface tension The stretchy 'skin' of a liquid, which is caused by the attraction between the tiny particles (molecules) on its surface.

Translucent Allowing light to pass through. Translucent substances bend and scatter the light so it is difficult to see objects clearly through them.

Transparent Allowing light rays to pass through. We can easily see through transparent substances.

Turbine A wheel with blades turned by the pressure of steam, water or gas. Turbines are used to drive ships, aircraft and the generators at power stations.

Ultra-violet ('Beyond the violet') Light Rays with a wavelength just shorter than the light at the violet end of the part of the spectrum we can see. Ultra-violet light is invisible to our eyes but other animals, such as bees can see it.

Water vapour Tiny droplets of water in air, which are so small you cannot see them. They are formed by evaporation.

Wavelength Various forms of energy (such as radiowaves, light and X-rays) travel in the form of waves. The wavelength is the distance between one wave and the next and it gives each type of energy its special properties.

Index

Page numbers in *italics* refer to illustrations or where illustrations and text occur on the same page.

Additional Illustrations:
Catherine Constable; pages 26–29, 42–45,
84–85, 116, 117, 162–165
Andrew Macdonald; pages 64–69, 72 (bottom left),
92, 93, 104, 105, 107 (top right)
Mike Saunders (*Jillian Burgess*); pages 52–53,
136–139, 154–161, 166
David Salariya and Shirley Willis; page 109 (bottom)
Crocker; pages 147, 153 (black and white)

Photographic Acknowledgements:
Argos Distributors Limited; 116
Blackpool Pleasure Beach, Astroswirl; 122
British Aerospace, Civil Aircraft Division; 71
J. Allan Cash; 13, 39, 78, 108, 139, 165
C.E.G.B.; 127
Michael Chinery; 163 (bottom)
Nik Cookson; 99, 103, 136
Warren Jepson Limited; 57
London Fire Brigade; 25
Nature Photographers; 77, 163 (top)
New York State, Commerce Department, Albany, N.Y.; 20
Osh Kosh Truck Corporation; 106
Parfums Lagerfeld Limited; 67
Port of Rotterdam; 35
R.O.S.P.A.; 156
Science Museum, London; 24, 142
Smiths Industries; 62
Thames Water; 42
Transport and Road Research Laboratory; 101
WHO Group; 167 (bottom)
ZEFA; 12, '17, 18, 41, 44, 46, (top and bottom), 52,
60–61, 72, 79, 80, 81, 84, 87, 95, 104, 112, 115,
126, 132, 135, 141, 159, 164, 167, (top)
Carl Zeiss Jena Limited; 145

Picture Research: Jackie Cookson